THE READER
IN THE PICARESQUE
NOVEL

HELEN H. REED

THE READER
IN THE PICARESQUE
NOVEL

TAMESIS BOOKS LIMITED
LONDON

Colección Támesis
SERIE A - MONOGRAFIAS, CXIV

Depósito legal: M. 38403-1984

Printed in Spain by Talleres Gráficos de SELECCIONES GRÁFICAS
Carretera de Irún, km. 11,500. Madrid-34

for
TAMESIS BOOKS LIMITED
LONDON

CONTENTS

ABBREVIATIONS

APCIH	Actas del Primer Congreso Internacional de Hispanistas.
BH	Bulletin Hispanique.
BHS	Bulletin of Hispanic Studies.
CHA	Cuadernos Hispanoamericanos.
HR	Hispanic Review.
KRQ	Kentucky Romance Quarterly.
MLN	Modern Language Notes.
MLR	Modern Language Review.
NRFH	Nueva Revista de Filología Hispánica.
PMLA	Publications of the Modern Language Association.
RF	Romanische Forschungen.
RR	Romanic Review.
YCGL	Yearbook of Comparative and General Literature.

(Y por si fueres pícaro, lector...»
(FRANCISCO DE QUEVEDO)

PREFACE

The source of inspiration for this study is to be found in the texts themselves, particularly the first chapter of *Guzmán de Alfarache,* in which the reader is immediately cast in an accusatory role vis-à-vis the narrator. I was impressed with the abiding presence of a fictitious reader in each of the works under consideration, and became curious regarding how this affected significance and the interpretations of actual readers past and present.

The present essay would never have reached fruition, however, without the help and encouragement of mentors, colleagues, friends, and relatives. First and foremost, I should like to thank Dr. Daniel Testa, the director of the dissertation upon which this book is based, for his excellent advice, guidance, and friendship. Equally valuable were the thoughtful suggestions of Dr. Rolena Adorno. I am grateful to Carmen Velasco and Jaime Ferrán for many pleasant conversations about Spanish literature through the years, to Dr. Demetrios Basdekis for his insights on existential criticism and the reader, and to Dr. Ignacio Izuzquiza, the «philosopher in the attic», for his wit and wisdom.

I gratefully acknowledge the financial assistance of Syracuse University, which provided a small grant to help defray publication expenses, and the aid of Robert C. Reed Jr. in preparing the final manuscript.

A special word of thanks is owed to my parents, Polly and Chauncey Hutchins, and to my sons, Jason and Cyrus, for their love, patience, and support through the many months devoted to research and writing.

Lastly, I particularly appreciate the help and encouragement of Professor Germán Bleiberg in bringing about the final text.

H. H. R.

January 1983

11

INTRODUCTION: THE CONCEPT OF THE READER AND ITS IMPLICATIONS FOR INTERPRETING THE PICARESQUE

Object of Study, Critical Assumptions, and Methodology

The purpose of this inquiry is to analyze the function of the reader-in-the-text in the semantic structures of three Spanish picaresque works of fiction: *La vida de Lazarillo de Tormes, Guzmán de Alfarache*, and *La vida del Buscón*. My assumption is that a writer fictionalizes an audience in his imagination while in the process of writing, and that this hypothetical reader or readers are manifest in the text itself[1]. As Henry James once remarked, «the author makes his reader very much as he makes his characters.»[2] My principal object of study is this literary creation of the reader in regard to his image, his roles, and his relationships with author, narrator, and real reader. The sort of reader the author is writing for and the nature of the responses he hopes to elicit are indicated in the prologues of picaresque works. How the author addresses the hypothetical or potential reader, shares with him narrative comment, and presents to him the illusory world represented in the fiction reveal this reader's appropriate role or stance as the narrative progresses. The way in which this hypothetical reader is called on to relate to the text indicates how the real reader should respond to the narrative material and ultimately interpret the work's significance.

My method of analysis will be based on a number of critical assumptions about the author, the text, the reader, and the process of writing. Briefly, the text is viewed as an indirect communication between author and reader, a message encoded by the author and decoded by the reader. It is only a potential work of art that is actualized in the process of being read.[3] Thus the reader is regarded as a necessary component in the creative process, which is ultimately an act of communication. The author writes with an

[1] See WALTER J. ONG, S.J.: «The Writer's Audience is Always a Fiction», *PMLA*, 90 (1975), 9-21.

[2] Quoted in WAYNE BOOTH: *The Rhetoric of Fiction* (Chicago and London: University of Chicago Press, 1961), p. 49.

[3] WOLFGANG ISER: «The Reading Process: A Phenomenological Approach», in *The Implied Reader* (Baltimore and London: Johns Hopkins University Press, 1974), pp. 274-294; STANLEY FISH: «Literature in the Reader: Affective Stylistics», in *Self-Consuming Artifacts* (Berkeley: University of California Press, 1972), pp. 381-427.

idea of his reader in mind and creates within the text a hypothetical reader to whom he is addressing the narration. Moreover, the fabric of the narrative will be affected by the author's perception of that reader's expected response. How a story is told reflects to whom it is being told. Consequently, content and style are inextricably bound to the nature of the audience they are determined for.

Both the author and reader assume roles and evolve personae in the text which may be distinguished from their existence outside the text. The writer *qua* man is not fully revealed in the text, but acquires a being more specialized and more apt to his function there. He creates his own role within the text and one for the reader as well, neither of which are fully identifiable with their complete selves. To distinguish these personae from the real author and real reader(s), one may refer to the author-in-the-text or implied author, and the reader-in-the-text or implied or hypothetical reader.[4] The real author is the actual writer himself —singular, corporeal, identifiable, and time-bound. The real reader is by necessity an abstract category, a phantom of the multitude of possible flesh and blood readers through history. The author will have projected his idea of a hypothetical reader in the text itself, but this image may be muddied by his inability to predict or impose uniformity on the composition of his readership, actual and potential. The character of the reader-in-the-text, therefore, is often one of the most ambiguous, nebulous, multiple, or even inconsistent of the author's creations.

The role and image of the hypothetical reader may be surmised from the way the author approaches the reader and the interpretive concepts introduced to the narration. The author tells the reader how to interpret in the prologue, through the use of significant chapter titles, by addressing him directly in the course of the narration, and by offering comment

---

[4] The critical studies on the image and the role of the reader are numerous, and there is little agreement on the terminology. For example, each of the fundamental studies cited below utilizes a different term to refer to the reader-in-the-text according to the perception of his function and relationship with the real reader. UMBERTO Eco in *The Role of the Reader: Explorations in the Semiotics of Text* (Bloomington-London: Indiana University Press, 1979) refers to a «model reader» who allows himself to be «manipulated by a complex text and its apparent structure and cooperates with the text spontaneously and without suspicion», in contrast to the analyst who sees beyond the author's stratagems. Eco stresses the essential control of text and codes over the reader's interpretation. The innocence of his model reader is markedly different from Iser's highly creative «implied reader» who responds to the author-narrator's expectations by actively participating in the generation of the text (WOLFGANG ISER: *The Implied Reader,* pp. 274-294). On the other hand, WALTER GIBSON's mock reader in «Authors, Speakers, Readers, and Mock Readers», *College English,* 9 (February 1950), 265-269, is an «artifact, controlled, simplified, abstracted» whose «mask and costume» the individual real reader takes on in order to appropriately experience the work. GERALD PRINCE in his «Introduction to the Study of the Narratee», in *Reader Response Criticism,* ed. Jane Tompkins (Baltimore and London: Johns Hopkins University Press, 1980), pp. 7-25, would reject the notion of the fictive reader as a second skin for the real reader to temporarily inhabit, since he stresses their very different identities. Since this is a problem I shall be alluding to periodically throughout my study, «hypothetical» reader seemed the term most free of critical connotations while still appropriate to my purposes.

directly or indirectly through one or more fictional characters. Even the language utilized in the text[5] indicates the appropriate role for the hypothetical reader, the way he is to perceive the reality depicted, and the interests and qualities he is (putatively) endowed with.

The hypothetical reader sometimes performs as an abstraction or textual structure, thereby inviting a mode of interpretation or proposing a perspective from which to view events. As Iser states in his discussion of the implied reader:

> Texts contain certain conditions of actualization that will allow their meaning to be assembled in the responsive mind of the recipient. The concept of the implied reader is therefore a textual structure anticipating the presence of a recipient without necessarily defining him: This concept prestructures the role to be assumed by each recipient and this holds true even when texts deliberately appear to ignore their possible recipient or actually exclude him. Thus the concept of the implied reader designates a network of response inviting structures, which impel the reader to grasp the text.[6]

The author-in-the-text may be clearly identified with the author's textual persona or may speak in the guise of one or several fictional narrators. Likewise the author may create a fictional character to play the role of the hypothetical reader. Often, however, he is not so specifically defined. He may be addressed in the narration directly as «reader», «friend», or through the use of second person form of address. Otherwise his presence, character, and tastes must be surmised from the way the text is presented, the questions answered, the imagery utilized, or the special concerns expressed.[7] More than one type of hypothetical reader may be present in the text, sometimes revealing differences between the author's preferences and expectations as far as his real readership is concerned. In dialogue itself the roles of speaker and listener alternate; fictional characters act and observe. The real reader as the ultimate *destinataire*[8] of the literary work must weigh his own reactions against the fictional readers, listeners, and spectators that react within the work — the fictional *destinataires* presented

---

[5] STEIN OLSEN: *The Structure of Literary Understanding* (Cambridge: Cambridge University Press, 1978), pp. 104 ff.

[6] WOLFGANG ISER: *The Act of Reading* (Baltimore and London: Johns Hopkins University Press, 1978), p. 34.

[7] PRINCE: «Introduction to the Study of the Narratee», pp. 7-25.

[8] I prefer the French term «destinataire» to «narratee» or «addressee» to refer to the persons addressed or narrated to, because it is the term first used by BÜLER and JAKOBSON in describing the various participants in the act of communication. (See OSWALD DUCROT and TZVETAN TODOROV: *Dictionnaire encyclopedique des sciences du langage* (Paris: Editions du Seuil, 1972), pp. 426, 427.) It is less specific than «addressee» since it applies equally well to the various roles —reader, listener, observer, spectator— that the «receiver» of a narration may be called upon to exercise. «Addressee» suggests a receptiveness to speech alone. The term «narratee» pales when used in conjunction with its more commonly used relative «narrator». Rather, I wanted to stress the importance and very existence of the receiver, to whom the narration is directed and for whom it was designed or even destined.

I have used *destinataire* as a broader term than hypothetical reader to refer to anyone designated to receive information within or outside the narration.

to him by the author. Whatever his guise within the narration, the hypothetical reader created by the author is indicative of one sort of reader he hopes for or expects; and he also serves as a fictional device whereby the author may direct or influence the real reader's response to his work. A relationship develops between the author-in-the-text and the reader-in-the-text in which the latter assumes characteristics and performs roles that the real reader must consider and may share. In all cases we are dealing with a series of narrative techniques through which the real author communicates his fiction to his audience, a scaffolding on which the artifice of the fiction rests.

My study of the image of the reader is complementary to one of point of view, but will focus on the completion of the communication process more than on its initiation. The emphasis is not on who narrates and from what perspective and with how much knowledge. Rather, the questions addressed are: 1) To whom is the narration directed and how does the author make that clear? 2) What role is the hypothetical reader(s) expected to play in regard to the narration? (Curious listener, snooper, kindred spirit, intimate friend, moralist, critical observer, hostile witness, and so on.) 3) From what distance does he view the events of the story? (Near, far, shifting.) 4) How does the hypothetical reader's anticipated response affect the process of the narration? 5) How does the hypothetical reader mediate between the text and the real reader? [9]

I have said that writing is both a process and an act of indirect communication, and that the work of art is ultimately realized in the reader. By the same token, the experience of reading is a process, the gradual reception of an indirect communication which is both immediately reacted to and later reflected upon. The study undertaken here departs from the methodology of the Formalists and New Critics and their assumption that the literary work is an object to be analyzed. Rather, a literary text consists of a sequence of verbal signs to be understood. Interpretation is less an autopsy to be performed than a choreography to be annotated. The reader undergoes an experience of the text while reading, during which in some way or another and with varying degrees of identification he relives the narrative, sometimes interrupted by reflections relating the text to extrinsic considerations and sometimes followed by a reflective experience. The competent reader is likely to consider the relationships between the various elements of the text and of the parts to the whole, what Todorov calls the «relations *in presentia*» or «intratextual relations».[10] He will also relate

[9] My questions have been devised with NORMAN FRIEDMAN's seminal article on point of view in mind («Point of View in Fiction: The Development of a Critical Concept», *PMLA*, LXX (December 1955). Point of view refers to the mode of presentation of a narration, and the role of the reader may be indicated to some degree as well, since whatever techniques the writer employs are to communicate the tale to the reader as effectively as possible. It follows that he will consider what the reader may respond to and form an image of the reader in his own mind. WAYNE BOOTH finds the concept «point of view» as it is traditionally used too limited to describe the many narrative devices of fiction. (*The Rhetoric of Fiction*, pp. 8-9.)

[10] TZVETAN TODOROV: *The Poetics of Prose* (Ithaca: Cornell University Press, 1977), pp. 242-244. For a detailed discussion of the act of reading, see a later portion of this chapter, pp. 34-35.

elements from the work in question to semantic systems outside the text itself—such as social codes, philosophic traditions, popular language, or literary conventions, which have been reflected or transformed within the text—i.e., the «relations *in absentia*» or «intertextual relations».[11] A seventeenth-century reader, for example, would share with the author knowledge of the literary genres and conventions of the period, of social systems and philosophical or religious ideas, and would interpret the significance of *Lazarillo* and *Guzmán* within the contexts of these systems; whereas a twentieth-century reader, after a long acquaintanceship with the novel, might respond primarily within the terms of that familiar genre. Thus, interpretations of a work may vary considerably from one historical period to another, and the author's message may not be decoded as he thought it would be.

The Reader in the Picaresque Novel

In the first picaresque novels, *Lazarillo* and *Guzmán,* the authors-in-the-text project a certain anxiety about the reaction of their potential readers, as well as uncertainty about their readers' identities, qualities, and tastes. Little is known with certainty about the sociological composition of the actual readership of the early picaresque novel.[12] One imagines a reading public comprised of aristocrats, courtiers, *conversos,* country gentry, the urban bourgeoisie, clergy, students, some women, and virtually no *pícaros.* Throughout Europe printing slowly democratized reading and brought the minor gentry and later the middle and lower classes into contact with written literature. Urban Spain underwent an educational revolution in the Sixteenth Century due to Fernando and Isabela's policy of recruiting civil servants from the middle classes.[13] It seems possible to postulate the

---

[11] TODOROV: *The Poetics of Prose,* p. 244. A detailed discussion of intertextuality and its usefulness both in elucidating the genesis of picaresque fiction and in making possible a variety of interpretations appears below, pp. 25-31.

[12] A sociological study of the relationship between fiction and the seventeenth-century Spanish reader, such as IAN WATT's *The Rise of the Novel* on eighteenth-century England, would be most valuable. A recent work, WALTER L. REED's *An Exemplary History of the Novel: the Quixotic versus the Picaresque* (London and Chicago: University of Chicago Press, 1981) suggests that WATT's criteria may be successfully applied to *Don Quijote* and the picaresque (pp. 20-22). Much of the work on the Spanish Golden Age readership emphasizes the insufficiency of the data. See, for example, MAXIME CHEVALIER: *Lectura y lectores en la España de los siglos XVI y XVII* (Madrid: Ediciones Turner, 1976); DANIEL EISENBERG: «Who Read the Romances of Chivalry», *KRQ,* XX (1973), 209-233; D. W. CRUICKSHANK: «Literature and the Booktrade in Golden Age Spain», *MLR,* LXXIII (1978), 799-824; and KEITH WHINNOM: «The Problem of the 'best-seller' in Spanish Golden-Age Literature», *BHS,* LVII (1980), 189-198. The present essay will deal with internal analysis of the works in question, more than with the historical evidence. Nonetheless, the question of who comprised the seventeenth-century readership seems worth posing and will remain a leitmotiv of this work. By characterizing the hypothetical reader addressed in the text, it may be possible to discover the public the author had in mind. (On this last point see ISER: *The Act of Reading,* p. 33.)

[13] CRUICKSHANK: «Literature and the Booktrade...», p. 811.

existence of a growing urban reading public. No doubt the individual novels varied in their appeal to different social groups as well as to different tastes, but the early picaresque novel might be described as a new genre in search of a readership, or a genre in the process of formation that created its own readership—when the political climate was ripe. After an initial success in 1554 and 1555, *Lazarillo* was banned by the Inquisition and suffered a long period of obscurity before it was republished with *Guzmán de Alfarache* in 1599.[14] The early years of the reign of Felipe III witnessed a burst of literary activity and relaxation of many of the strictures imposed during the rule of his father.

Guzmán was an authentic best seller for its time and was widely imitated, yet it evoked a negative response from some contemporary writers. This is quite understandable when one considers the controversial and innovative nature of the material. As the anonymous author of *Lazarillo* remarks in the prologue: «los gustos no son todos unos.» Most picaresque authors ostensibly cater to more than one type of reader, possibly reflecting the widening sociological spectrum of the reading public the works were destined for. Mateo Alemán addresses two antithetical sorts of readers in his prologue—the discreet reader and the *vulgo*. This distinction was initiated by Alemán, and became a convention of Golden Age prologues. Writers consistently maligned *el vulgo,* but may have deferred to that sector of the reading public more than they imply.[15] Be that as it may, picaresque writers seem to have expected some variety in their readership. Even a work as late as *Estebanillo González* pays tribute to the wide spectrum of readers it is designed to please, so that the reader is addressed as «carísimo o muy barato o quienquiera que tú fueres», and later as «lampiño o barbudo lector o quienquiera que fueres.»

Thus, the initial works of the picaresque genre are directed to a reader that is somewhat ambiguously defined, though he acquires an intimate knowledge of the *pícaro*'s life. The author of *Lazarillo* alludes to various types of readers and readings in the prologue, and Lazarillo addresses his confession to a fictitious reader, the anonymous «Vuestra Merced,» whose presence determines the shape of the narration in a number of ways. Mateo Alemán specifies the qualities of an ideal reader in the prologue in contrast to the *vulgo* he so fears and reviles, but the reader Guzmán exhorts, cajoles, criticizes, harangues, apologizes to, and accuses during the course of the narration seems less than «discreet» and even prone to the bad reading tastes and moral fallibility of the *vulgo*. In both works the *pícaro* seemingly selects his material and modifies his account in deference to the hypothetical reader(s). At the same time the real reader is manipulated by the use of other narrative techniques to closely experience the adventures of the *pícaro* and to sympathize with the problematic nature of the *pícaro*'s life. The reason that *Lazarillo* and *Guzmán* may be considered precursors of the novel owes much to the way the *pícaro*'s experience is shared with

---

[14] CLAUDIO GUILLÉN: *Literature as System* (Princeton: Princeton University Press, 1971), pp. 137-143.
[15] CRUICKSHANK: «Literature and the Booktrade...», pp. 818-824.

the reader. I shall devote a chapter to each of these early picaresque works in order to elucidate the function of the hypothetical reader(s) in each text's interpretation.

Subsequent early readers of the picaresque encountered a different reading experience, because by the early Seventeenth Century both authors and readers were familiar with the initial works of picaresque fiction, a fact which is acknowledged in the prologues. Chapter IV will deal with Quevedo, and in my conclusion I shall make brief mention of Cervantes by way of contrast with the other works. Both Quevedo and Cervantes imitated, transformed, and at times even rejected the conventions of the inchoate genre initiated by *Guzmán* and *Lazarillo*. The *Buscón* is in many ways a parody of the picaresque and, as such, makes demands different from those imposed on the readers of earlier works. The work is ostensibly written as a book of jokes to amuse the nobility and to sell well (see prologue), and may be interpreted as both a parody and political rejection of the *pícaro's* aspirations. In addressing the reader, Quevedo seems to vacillate between the conventions of *Lazarillo* and *Guzmán,* possibly because their function in eliciting a certain type of reader involvement is not important in the *Buscón*. The *pícaro* is displayed and distanced from both author and reader, more of a gesticulating silhouette than the teller of an intimate tale. The figuration of the prose often repeats in miniature the archetypical picaresque experience of being humiliated—hyperbole followed by sudden undercutting. The reader's attention is mostly drawn to a surface of conceits and grotesque visual images, rather than the *pícaro's* problematic existence, which assumes secondary importance to the show of verbal virtuosity. Here my object is not only to describe the role of the hypothetical reader and how that affects the real reader's interpretation of the work, but also to clarify how its function differs, if it does, in *Lazarillo* and *Guzmán.*

Whereas Quevedo's Don Pablos is predestined to remain mired in his picaresque way of life, Cervantes' *pícaros* freely embark on their adventures like actors assuming roles. The reader is held at a distance, a detached witness to a dialogue between *pícaro* and *pícaro,* rather than a participant in an implied dialogue that takes place between reader and *pícaro*. His narrations are presented to the reader like tableaux, in which the distinction between narrator and spectator becomes blurred, because their roles are often exchanged. At the same time, Cervantes approaches the reader on a metalinguistic level as a fellow reader and kindred spirit, an equal who must share the author's literary knowledge to appreciate his playfulness and the multitude of ironies with which he undermines the fiction of his predecessor, Mateo Alemán. Cervantes creates an idle reader («desocupado lector») to be entertained at his leisure. The author's voice remains elusive and not readily identifiable among the multitude of narrators. By the same token, the reader is granted a high degree of autonomy and is left free to interpret as he will. In contrast, Mateo Alemán virtually bombards the reader with the intensely emotional accusations of a single narrator and appears to exercise a high degree of control over his responses. For the purposes of this study I shall only regard Cervantes as a perceptive

19

ic of the picaresque, and make use of his recognition and rejection of narrative techniques adopted by other practitioners of the genre.

Although certain conventions developed in the way the reader was addressed in picaresque fiction, it is evident from the previous remarks that the role of the reader varies considerably from novel to novel. My study will describe and interpret both the conventions and the variations. I suspect, for example, that writers who parody the *pícaro* tend to accommodate their narrations to the nobility, and that novels which offer a sympathetic and serious treatment of the *pícaro* reflect greater ambiguity in their approach to the reader. Thus the way in which the reader is addressed has ideological as well as artistic implications, due no doubt to the controversial and problematic nature of the *pícaro* as a character in fiction.

The «Pícaro» as a Literary Character, and Renaissance Society

The picaresque novel is the pseudo-autobiography of an orphan who becomes a rogue. The *pícaro* is born in dishonor and poverty to parents that he abandons at an early age. He is obliged to fend for himself in a world of tricksters, whom he observes and to some degree imitates in order to survive. The *pícaro* of the Sixteenth and Seventeenth Centuries is a novel fictional character not unrelated to a novel social type that emerged in the burgeoning cities of Spain, a fortune seeker of low birth with few social or family ties who tried to better his lot in the anonymity of the city. The urban poverty and increase in vagabondage provide a historical corollary to the new literary character.[16] The *pícaro* in literature and in life represented a controversial novelty in a period of social change and instability. Social unrest was not confined to the lower classes, and the feelings and life experience of the literary *pícaro* might have been shared in one way or another by three groups who found themselves in an anomalous position in seventeenth-century Spain: the urban poor, the *converso,* and the newly poor country gentleman.[17] Many individuals from these classes were unable to find a social role appropriate to their ambition or status or financial need. Readers who had suffered alienation or economic frustration or fear of such might have understood the *pícaro*'s experience either as correlative to their own or as a frightening possibility.

[16] JAVIER HERRERO: «Renaissance Poverty and Lazarillo's Family: The Birth of the Picaresque Genre», *PMLA,* 94 (Oct. 1979), 876-886. DEREK W. LOMAX in «On Re-reading the *Lazarillo de Tormes*», in *Studia iberica: Festschrift für Hans Flasche* (Bern: Francke, 1973), pp. 371-381, discusses the contrast between wealth and poverty in a period of prosperity and political expansion, and the resulting revolution of rising expectations. On the increase in poverty, vagrancy, and banditry in Renaissance Spain, see FERNAND BRAUDEL: *The Mediterranean and the Mediterranean World in the Age of Philip II,* vol. II, trans. Siân Reynolds (London: Collins, 1972), 734-756; and JACQUES SOMBEROUX: «Pauvreté et Marginalité», *Imprévue* (1980-1981), pp. 9-21. On the relationship between picaresque literature and society see PETER DUNN: *The Spanish Picaresque Novel* (Boston: Twayne, 1979), pp. 139-145.
[17] CLAUDIO GUILLÉN: *Literature as System,* pp. 101, 144; FRANCISCO RICO: *La Novela Picaresca Española* (Barcelona: Planeta, 1967), pp. xxxiii-xxxix.

20

The lack of a secure social role partially explains the psychology of the *pícaro,* who is socially, and therefore «ontologically», insecure.[18] The *pícaro* is a dissembler, forever performing a role in which he is inevitably unmasked, discovered as a fraud, and rejected. His self is fashioned by the events of his life, i.e., by the accumulation of rejections and the necessity to keep on performing in order to survive. Readers are presented with a mode of existence whose instability would have been infrequently experienced in the feudal social order of the Middle Ages, except briefly during carnival time—when the mighty were symbolically brought down by the satire of the lowly who temporarily assumed their places. The *pícaro's* activities reflect carnivalistic structures, but the spirit and meaning of his comicity are difficult to interpret. He attempts to make permanent for himself the sort of social reverses traditionally enacted in those carnival rituals which provided catharsis, amusement, and temporary relief from the hierarchical class system. The *pícaro* does not accept his low place in the social hierarchy and defines himself according to his ambitions. At the same time the rich and powerful are satirized, and thus brought down from their lofty pedestal. The *pícaro* masks himself and unmasks others. His desire —often unfulfilled— is to bring the high low and elevate the low (himself). As a social anomaly and a symbol of change and reversal, the *pícaro* is of necessity a controversial literary figure.[19]

The central theme or problem to which the picaresque genre is devoted is the social rise of the *pícaro* or the search of the *pícaro* for a place *in* society, certainly a novel enterprise in early narrative. The contrast becomes more marked when one considers the differences between the picaresque and other genres of Renaissance narrative. In contrast to the epic where the hero ventures forth *in behalf of* society, or romance where the hero sets out in quest of some far-off, otherwordly, mysterious goal *outside* society, the *pícaro's* aim is limited in scope, egotistical, ignoble, and of this world —to have enough money and food to survive and to find a place *within* society. The locus or space of the picaresque novel is greatly reduced in comparison to the epic or romance of chivalry, and offers an ironic contrast. Paradoxically, the *pícaro* is often unable to achieve his aim —seemingly within his reach yet ever elusive— while the romance hero reaches for and grasps the impossible. The emotion formalized in romance is longing fulfilled. The affective structure of the picaresque is often frustration, but a frustration counter-balanced by a sense of renewal and hope in the

[18] R. D. LAING: *The Divided Self* (1959 rpt. Baltimore: Penguin Books, 1965), pp. 39-61.
[19] The carnivalization of literature is a favorite theme of BAKHTIN in both *Problems of Dostoevsky's Poetics* (U.S.A.: Ardis, 1973), pp. 83-149, and *Rabelais and his World* (Cambridge, Mass. and London, England: The M.I.T. Press, 1965). EDMOND CROS in *L'Aristocrate et Le Carnaval des Geux* (Montpeller: Publication du Centre d'Etude Sociocritiques V.E.R. II, Université Paul Valéry, 1975) has applied Bakhtin's ideas about carnivalization to the *Buscón;* MANUEL DURÁN in «El Quijote a través del prisma de Mikhail Bakhtine: Carnaval, disfraces, escatología y locura», in *Cervantes and the Renaissance,* ed. Michael D. McGaha (Easton, Pennsylvania: Juan de la Cuesta, 1980) discusses carnivalistic structures and the *Quijote.*

21

new mask and the new role. The reader shares in the ideals presented through the hero of the epic, escapes from society into the land of magic and daydream with romance, but is faced with the contradictions within society in the picaresque novel. Generally, the historical progression of narrative genres —epic to romance to picaresque— seems to function in relation to societal values in an increasingly deleterious manner. The epic integrates and upholds the values of society, and acts as a force of social cohesion. Romance offers individual escape into fantasy. The picaresque presents social criticism and confrontation without solution. Here narrative has become problematic, and the reader's role in interpretation far more demanding.

Modern Fiction and the Picaresque: One Cause of Misreadings

As a fictional character, the *pícaro* was not only amusing, controversial, and problematical to contemporary readers, but may be considered as a prototype that has periodically and consistently re-emerged in various guises in fiction up to the present. Thus, one recent trend has been to characterize the picaresque novel according to its similarities with certain works of modern fiction. Hindsight informs our interpretation of the picaresque as precursor to those modern novels that deal with an alienated and peripatetic anti-hero who can find no place for himself in society. According to this view, the picaresque hero exemplifies a certain *Weltanschauung*—an anguished state of non-belonging with which the sensitive and disillusioned modern reader is expected to readily identify. The *pícaro*, like many protagonists of contemporary novels, is involved in what Claudio Guillén, following Henry James, calls a tangle.[20] He is an individual in conflict with his environment. His efforts at social integration and coming to terms with his environment repeatedly fail, and his life assumes, therefore, a pattern in which he is rejected or he himself rejects his present situation and begins again at something else—like Sisyphus ever pushing his great boulder up the mountain only to watch it tumble down again from the summit. The action of the picaresque novel is repetitious and consists of a series of frustrations and humiliations for the *pícaro*.

Some picaresque novels —notably *Lazarillo* and *Guzmán de Alfarache*— conform nicely to this model, but other seventeenth-century picaresque works differ in their mood and significance. Therefore to characterize the historical genre from this twentieth-century perspective both limits its scope and falsifies the nature of its beginnings. Synchronically the picture was quite different, although Guillén's diachronic vision of the genre establishes what survived and what is most congenial to modern taste. Many seventeenth-century *pícaros* are not as dreary and depressed as some modern anti-heroes, and are more comic than tragic or pathetic characters. It is misleading to stress only the Sisyphean dilemma of the *pícaro*, his rebuffs and failure, rather than his sense of humor, resilience, and resource-

---

[20] GUILLÉN: *Literature as System*, p. 77.

fulness. Modern interpretations tend to underplay these merits of the *pí-caro*'s peculiar psychological configuration.

The predominant interest of the picaresque novel is social, and the relationship of the *pícaro* to society is the key consideration. What varies considerably in the Seventeenth Century is the author's attitude toward his protagonist, which may or may not be shared by the reader. The reaction of both author and reader to the *pícaro* and his rise in society as it is recorded in fiction is diverse and many-faceted. Great significance has been attached to the fact that the picaresque novel is written from a first person point of view and thus a singular and even dogmatic perspective.[21] But it should also be noted that the author's voice does not always correspond to the *pícaro*'s. The *pícaro* judges the world, and the author and the reader judge the *pícaro*. Some writers view the *pícaro* with sympathy, others with ironic detachment, amusement, or even disapproval and dislike. Within each novel itself the *pícaro* may produce a variety of responses. The historical genre is too often confused with what has been called the «picaresque myth»,[22] and is reduced to a description of those picaresque novels that sympathetically and seriously treat the adventures of an outsider or anti-hero. I would contend that even those novels are more ambiguous in their presentation of the *pícaro* than the aforementioned view would indicate. In the Seventeenth Century, the *pícaro* and his problematic relationship to society inspired highly diverse reactions. Psychological interpretations of the *pícaro* varied considerably, as did the political and social ideology of the novels. The *pícaro* is not only a precursor of the modern anti-hero, the reader's alter-ego, but also of the oft-satirized social climber or *parvenu*. He is a descendent as well of the medieval trickster and the carnival clown.

The Narrative Tradition and The Nature of Relationships Between Works

The years 1599-1606 witnessed a particularly intense literary activity in Spain. Many major picaresque works were written, and there seems to have been a dialectical or dialogical relationship among the texts.[23] They answer to one another and as such constitute a system. To make a linguistic analogy,[24] the individual works in the development of a genre or the lit-

[21] CARLOS BLANCO AGUINAGA: «Cervantes y la Picaresca. Notas sobre dos tipos de realismo», *NRFH*, XI (1957), 313-342.
[22] Cf. GUILLÉN: *Literature as System*, pp. 99-100; and ALEXANDER BLACKBURN: *The Myth of the Pícaro* (Chapel Hill: The University of North Carolina Press, 1979), pp. 3-35.
[23] On the self-conscious and self-referential quality of the genre, see HOWARD MANCING: «The Picaresque Novel: A Protean Form», *College Literature*, VI (1979-1980), 182-184.
[24] Saussure's *langue/parole* distinction has been used as a model to oppose structure and event, or system and process in the description of various cultural, historical, and literary phenomena. For some examples, see: ROLAND BARTHES: *Elements of Semiology* (New York: Hill and Wang, 1967), pp. 13-32, and RENÉ WELLEK and AUSTIN WARREN: *Theory of Literature*, 3d. ed. (1963 rpt. London: Penguin, 1976), p. 152.

erature of a generation of writers may be thought of as *speech acts* which partake of a common *langue*. *Langue* is the realm of possibilities that the individual speech acts never entirely exhaust. *Langue* may also be thought of as a system of enabling conventions that allow the process of speech acts or the practice of the genre. But the individual works of the picaresque genre answer to one another sharply. They do not agree. The constants that unite many of the works are subject and form—i.e., they are generally the episodic autobiography of a *pícaro,* but the differences in attitude regarding the *pícaro* and his place in society are enormous.[25]

Indeed, the relationships between texts treating the theme of the picaresque seem quite different from the relationships between the texts in many genres of the Middle Ages and Renaissance, where the basic ideas and feelings expressed remain relatively constant. The form and meaning of the epic, romance, saint's life, moral example, sentimental novel, and pastoral novel do not substantially change, although they contain an almost infinite number of small variations. In the Baroque Age, filiation by imitation and amplification is less frequent than irony, antithesis, transformation, and transgression.[26] The medieval respect for tradition offers a marked contrast to the literary rivalry of the Golden Age, and many writers included criticism and abuse of contemporary writers and contemporary literary works in their texts. The picaresque genre developed through a debate on a problematical issue —the *pícaro's* relationship to society— with parody and irony as frequent means of argumentation. The individual works posit fundamental political differences, and each author tries in one way or another to persuade the reader of the truth of his vision.

The urge to parody, which involves a mocking of, a turning away from, or a relativization of, is a natural tendency when one is confronted with an

[25] In order to situate the works in question in a wider context it may be useful to recall the following classification of picaresque fiction devised by RICHARD BJORNSON in *The Picaresque Hero in European Fiction* (Madison: The University of Wisconsin Press, 1977), p. 70. He divides picaresque novels into the four following categories:

1. Works in which the *pícaro* is parodied, such as *La Pícara Justina* and *El Buscón.*

2. Works that «retain the morally serious tone, autobiographical perspective, and encyclopedic tendencies of MATEO ALEMÁN's *Guzmán de Alfarache».* Included in this group would be the *Guzmán apócrifo* by JUAN MARTÍ, *Marcos de Obregón* by VICENTE ESPINEL, and *El donado hablador, Alonso: Mozo de muchos amos* by JERÓNIMO DE ALCALÁ YÁÑEZ Y RIBERA.

3. Works that entertain and underplay the more problematical aspects of the *pícaro's* life, such as the picaresque adventure stories of Salas Barbadillo and Castillo Solórzano.

4. Socially critical novels written by exiles like JUAN DE LUNA, author of *La segunda parte de Lazarillo de Tormes,* and CARLOS GARCÍA, author of *La desordenada codicia de los bienes ajenos.*

Although these categories may describe the dominant features of some picaresque works, they should not be considered as mutually exclusive. I mention them in passing to give an idea of the variety in and later development of the genre and to place the works I will be treating in a wider context.

[26] LAURENT JENNY in «La Strategie de la forme», *Poetique,* 27 (1976), 257-281 categorizes the possible relationships of a literary work to its archetypal model as realization, transformation, or transgression.

extreme position. As Kenneth Burke has remarked, «the greater the absolutism of the statements, the greater the subjectivity and relativity of the position of the agent making the statements.» [27] The very absence of irony makes romance or epic susceptible to irony and provided, no doubt, one impetus for the genesis of picaresque narrative. Similarly, the picaresque novel of Mateo Alemán is an extreme statement and as such provoked a variety of ironic reactions. *Lazarillo* may be interpreted as an anti-romance, and some works of Cervantes as partially anti-picaresque. It may be true that the fundamental motives for parody have not varied much in literary history, but the forms of parody and the play of parodic elements in the formation of new ideological constructions are more difficult to characterize. Parody may serve as an end in itself or a point of departure, and seems to function in both senses in the composition of all picaresque works.

The dialectical or polemical development of the picaresque genre has important implications for the readers of these fictions. The effect of these works in the reader is of great resonance, demanding his thought and active participation in resolving the fictions's dilemmas. Indeed, the term «dialectical» may be applied to the process of reading these texts, to the way the reader is induced to respond to them. Stanley Fish distinguishes between what he calls «rhetorical and dialectical presentation in fiction.» The former presents or mirrors the familiar world the reader already knows, approves of, and holds to be true. The latter challenges and disturbs accepted systems of knowledge, and requires that the reader search for a new truth himself. The first type of reading experience flatters the reader and reinforces his beliefs. The second unsettles the reader and perhaps converts him to a new way of thinking. [28] The three works under consideration in this study probably pertain to the latter category, yet at the same time approach the reader in fundamentally different ways through their very different techniques in the creation of the fictitious and/or hypothetical readers.

The Validity of Intertextuality for the Study of the Picaresque

My approach is not only based on the myriad recent studies on the image and role of the reader in various literary forms, but also on the bold ideas of the Russian Formalist Bakhtin which were later amplified and elaborated by Julia Kristeva and others to establish a mode of criticism commonly designated as «intertextual». Particularly useful for my analysis are Bakhtin's early studies of what he calls «the double-voiced word», i.e., a word which is not only «directed toward the object of speech, but contains clear reference to another word, toward another person's speech.» [29]

---

[27] KENNETH BURKE: «Four Master Tropes», in *A Grammar of Motives* [1945] (reprint, Berkeley and Los Angeles: University of California Press, 1969), p. 512.
[28] STANLEY FISH: *Self-Consuming Artifacts* (Berkeley: University of California Press, 1972), pp. 1-4.
[29] MIKHAIL BAKHTIN: *Problems of Dostoevsky's Poetics* (USA: Ardis, 1973), p. 153.

Bakhtin develops an entire taxonomy of double-voiced words and the situations where they occur, but only some of these need concern us here. He refers explicitly, for example, to the effect of a reader's anticipated response to a writer's prose and thus the presence of an implicit or hidden polemic that will influence the direction of the writing. «Any literary word is more or less keenly aware of its listener, reader, or critic, and reflects in itself his anticipated objections, assessments, and points of view.» [30] Other types of «double-directedness» encountered in literary texts are parody, stylization, and any instance in which a reference to a pre-existing literary text makes itself felt in the work in question. Intertextual critics have made literary the oral orientation of the terminology of Bakhtin, and speak of «texts» rather than «voices», and of the reminiscences of texts within other texts. The concept of a text has been broadened to include extra-literary structures, such as social or semantic systems and cultural contexts, and their effect on literary structures has also been studied. A basic assumption of this critical apparatus is the «double-voiced» or polysemic nature of words.

The implicit presence of «voices» other than that of the *pícaro*-protagonist in the picaresque novel seemed to me unmistakeable. Because of their innovative nature, the earliest picaresque novels appear to have been written with the reaction of the potential reader very much in mind. Those that followed were in part readers' (turned writers) responses to the earlier novels. There are sufficient grounds to indicate that any writer of picaresque fiction in the early Seventeenth Century must have been familiar with *Guzmán* or *Lazarillo* or both. Any writer of the picaresque novel was necessarily a reader of same, and in his own version of the picaresque would somehow record his response as a reader to his predecessors. A literary work is not only orientated toward its potential readers, but also toward pre-existing literary works.

A novel, Julia Kristeva has written, is a sum of texts and a structure of transformation.[31] It will contain reminiscences and citations from earlier works, which will be transformed in their new context and imbued with new meaning, for they form part of a new signifying system. Intertextuality approaches reading and writing as a process, rather than what is written as a static object. «It provides us with a model in which a literary structure does not exist on its own, but rather is elaborated in relationship to another structure.» [32] («Un modèle où la structure littéraire *n'est pas,* mais où elle s'élabore par rapport à une autre structure.») A novel is elaborated in its relationship to the reader and in its relationship to selected literary texts of the past. By the same token, reading is a process and the experience of reading is intertextual, inseparable from the remembrance of past texts and the reader's particular knowledge and experience.

Intertextual criticism is not only a method of doing literary criticism,

[30] BAKHTIN: *Problems of Dostoevsky's Poetics,* p. 162.

[31] JULIA KRISTEVA: *Le Texte du Roman* (The Hague and Paris: Mouton, 1970), pp. 149-176.

[32] KRISTEVA: *Semiotiké: Recherches pour une sémanalyse* (Paris: Seuil, 1969), p. 144.

but also a method of doing literary history, because it clarifies the nature of relationships between texts. Historians make use of cause and effect to weave isolated facts into a coherent story that explains what happened and why. Texts in the system of literary history are like events in the system of history. They are the material of literary history that must be given form and understood in their connection to each other.

Intertextuality provides an approach to literary history that is dialectical rather than organic. By that I mean that it gives equal status to a negative influence or rejection of a literary norm or convention on the one hand, and to the persistence of tradition on the other. One aim of intertextual criticism is to accurately describe the way in which a text is incorporated into another. The nineteenth-century concentration on source studies and search for origins led to a view of literary history in which each development emanated from an earlier *source*. This watery metaphor subtly informed literary studies, which have concentrated on the forward «flow» of a tradition. Concurrently, negative influences or anti-traditions and the place of parody in literary history were underestimated. Yet many writers elaborate their own works in relation to structures they ostensibly reject. As Guillén states: «negative impacts or influence *à rebours,* through which a norm is dialectically surpassed (and assimilated) by another, or a genre by a counter-genre, constitute one of the main ways in which a literary model acts upon a writer.» [33]

Such a dynamic is surely evident in the development of the picaresque genre. Some works of picaresque fiction are constructed *via* a series of negativities in opposition to past literary models as well as to contemporary social mores. Parody and satire are important principles of composition, and the mode or figuration of this fiction is often ironic. The positive influence exercised by renewed contact with classical literature during the Renaissance was accompanied by an aggressively negative response to the literature of the immediate past. Rejection of medieval models is the counterpart of a desire to imitate the classics, and both tendencies were in evidence in the formation of new literary works. In general, a work that is highly innovative like *Lazarillo* is apt to display a negative attitude toward some of its immediate antecedents, and to provoke an equally strong reaction in some of the works that follow. The dynamics of the development of the genre might be described as dialectical or dialogical in that each new work seems to answer to its predecessors. Indeed, the arena of the debate might better be enlarged to include all fiction of the period and even that other mode of representation, *la comedia.*

---

[33] GUILLÉN: *Literature as System,* p. 146. The importance of negativity has also been stressed by ANNA BALAKIAN in her analysis of the nature of influences, «Influence and Literary Fortune: The Equivocal Junction of two Methods», *YCGL,* 11 (1962), 24-31; and by the post-Freudian critic HAROLD BLOOM in his discussions of the role of rebellion and psychic defenses in literary relationships, *The Anxiety of Influence* (New York: Oxford University Press, 1973) and *A Map of Misreading* (New York: Oxford University Press, 1975). Some modern writers are, of course, quite explicit in their negativity; consider, for example, the anti-novel of JULIO CORTÁZAR and the anti-poetry of NICANOR PARRA.

Traditional source criticism looked too closely and too exclusively at links between one literary work and another, and gave clear preference to establishing similarities rather than specifying whatever changes may have occurred. Intertextual criticism attempts to clarify the *relationship* that exists between two works or between the work and system of norms we designate as genre. The significance of a literary text is partly determined by the way it incorporates reminiscences from earlier works. The new text may realize possibilities inherent to, but not fully developed in the «prototype», metamorphoze forms and details, rob an element of its original meaning or place in the literary structure, imbue a tired convention with new significance, or underplay or exaggerate features and attributes. An author may wholeheartedly embrace, qualify, criticize, mock, or parody portions of past texts. Intertextual criticism evaluates both what is incorporated into the new text and how it is treated there. The Nineteenth Century seemed most concerned with the reproduction or repetition of elements. But the writer is not limited to duplicating reality like a photographer. He may reproduce, develop and refine, transform, reject, or transgress the features and patterns of earlier literary texts.

Because of its elegance, intertextuality provides a viable means of analyzing various aspects of the picaresque novel and novels.[34] For one thing, one can be virtually certain that picaresque novels following *Lazarillo* and *Guzmán* make reference to them, and thus the primary difficulty of identification is lessened, if not entirely removed.[35] The historical period, the Sixteenth and Seventeenth Centuries in Spain, is one that produced an abundance of the sort of self-conscious and self-critical literature that intertextual critics delight in analyzing. Picaresque fiction is only one example of this phenomenon. Others are Quevedo's numerous parodies of heroic «romances», or his sonnets on irreverent subjects. In order to appreciate these works we must consider the original work «in filigram» (as Severo Sarduy puts it) within the present text,[36] or be aware of the conventions of the romance and the sonnet. Cervantes' work abounds in intertextual playfulness of an exceedingly complex nature. In the *Quijote* alone, it is quite easy to identify the parody of many particular genres of Medieval and Renaissance fiction including, of course, the most obvious—the books of chivalry.

---

[34] PETER DUNN has recently suggested the value of an intertextual approach to the study of the picaresque genre and proposes to write a book on the subject. See «Problems of a model for the picaresque and the case of Quevedo's *Buscón*», *BHS*, LIX (1982), 95-105. The present study was written before I was acquainted with Dunn's article.

[35] A difficulty inherent to intertextual criticism is the primary task of recognition in all but the most obvious instances, i.e., where a text or portion of a text exactly duplicates another. Often we do not know whether an author has entered into a dialogue with a specific work or passage, or is responding to a convention or a set of conventions and therefore an abstract and hypothetical construct of which he is consciously or even unconsciously aware.

[36] SEVERO SARDUY: «El Barroco y el Neobarroco», in *América Latina en su literatura*, ed. César Fernández Moreno, 3d. ed. (Unesco, 1972; rpt. México: Siglo Veintiuno, 1976), p. 176.

The *Quijote* and some picaresque works are often cited as precursors of the novel. Modern fiction is not naive like a myth or medieval romance or a folktale. We are not presented with paradigms only, although these never entirely disappear, but also with departures from paradigms. Indeed, Bakhtin bases his theory of the novel on its anti-canonical nature,[37] and Frank Kermode has pointed out that one essential element of modern fiction is «peripeteia», the presence of the unexpected. We are not certain how a novel will end or how the protagonist will resolve or fail to resolve his particular difficulties. The novel does not have the sense of a predetermined ending which governs and regulates its form. The novel is problematic and the solution is worked out in the telling.[38] Both the picaresque novel and the *Quijote* have difficulty in ending. The *pícaro,* as Ginés de Pasamonte in the *Quijote* points out, cannot stop recounting his life, because it is not over yet. Any pause in the Sisyphus rhythm of the action either at the top of the mountain or at the bottom gives an erroneous idea of the conclusion of the *pícaro*'s adventures, which death will terminate, perhaps without any substantial improvement in his fortune or acceptance into society. No Penelope, homeland, or even reward awaits the *pícaro* at the end of the journey. The picaresque novel is, in this sense, open-ended. Each individual picaresque novel ends a little differently, which shows, I think, that there was not a set or easy solution in this regard. The *Quijote,* on the other hand, forces upon us the unpalatable. The *Quijote* should never end, as Unamuno suggested, because we do not want the dream of heroism and perfection to be negated.[39] In neither case are we dealing with an archetypal genre of fiction such as those produced in the medieval period. In many forms of fiction the conclusion is predictable and to a large degree even determines the form of that which precedes it. One knows what to expect from a folktale, romance, epic, saint's life, or tragedy —resolution and closure. The picaresque novel and the *Quijote* represent conflicts of a philosophical and social nature not so easily resolved in a narrative structure, and therefore not so easily interpreted by the reader. Open-endedness and the demands on the reader's active participation in arriving at the work's significance distinguish the novel from earlier forms of fiction.

Intertextual criticism has been successfully used to explore some differences between Renaissance and Medieval literature, which further substantiate the dichotomy posited by Kermode between naive and sophisticated fiction and by Fish between rhetorical and dialectical presentation (see p. 25). Particularly illuminating are Julia Kristeva's study, *Le Texte du Roman,* and an article by Paul Zumthor, «Le Carrefour des Rhetoriqueurs». Both critics discuss the abandonment of the conservative and traditional literary norms of the Middle Ages, of a philosophical system

---

[37] BAKHTIN: *The Dialogic Imagination* (Austin: The University of Texas Press, 1981).

[38] FRANK KERMODE: *The Sense of an Ending* (Oxford: Oxford University Press, 1966), pp. 18, 19; 35-64.

[39] MIGUEL DE UNAMUNO: *Vida de Don Quijote y Sancho,* 6th ed. (Buenos Aires and México: Espasa-Calpe Argentina, S. A., 1945), p. 265.

regarded as eternal, of the paradigmatic knowledge that rested its authority on the past and its universal acceptance. Discourse in the Middle Ages respected a series of rhetorical rules and provided models which could be reproduced, embellished, amplified, and even parodied, but whose authority remained essentially unchallenged. The decorated manuscripts of the IXth Century were sacred in that they symbolized the word of God and hence the divine law. The book was a sacred and magical object—even a fetish. Gradually the book lost its divine and ossified status, concerned itself with the production of significance and not with the presentation of the eternal, lost its status as symbol and became the vehicle for a culture concerned with signs. The novel is a product of the nominalist mentality, thinking, doubting, intellectualizing, no longer concerned with perpetuating universals, searching now for particular truths. The novel concerns the quest of an individual for relative values, for a personal solution. The novel is a sum of books, «une juxtaposition infinie d'énoncés nonhierarchisés.» Discourse is no longer symbolic. There is no universal idea or fundamental truth that it exemplifies or justifies.[40]

Intertextual criticism seems an appropriate mode of interpretation with which to unravel some of the complexity of the novel, and comprehensively define a work's meaning.[41]. Understanding is derived from studying a text in its relationship to others, whereby the critic is provided with a variety of perspectives on the subject in question, which is seen as an integral part of various systems. The notion of what constitutes a text is broad and might include the spoken language, social structures, cultural contexts, and non-verbal systems contemporary with the work under study. Thus the text is situated within a number of frameworks, and questions such as tone, value, and attitude are also considered. Moreover, the subtleties in the relationship between a fiction and its predecessors or paradigm are described. A genre is no longer viewed as a taxonomic concept, but rather as a system of possibilities, modulated by or realized in each particular work.[42]

Intertextuality has led to a better grasp of works that are in part parodies of an earlier work. A parody is «polysemic» and sophisticated, for it introduces a semantic direction to the new work that is diametrically opposed to the original text's intention,[43] and induces the reader to recognize the ambiguities of experience and of language. Parody is both a critical and creative act. It is likely to question the values inherent to the

---

[40] KRISTEVA: *Le Texte du Roman*, pp. 19-31.

[41] Since the novel is a complex form of fiction, the structural approach initiated by Vladimir Propp on the morphology of the Russian folktale and the search for the deep structures of myth of Claude Lévi-Strauss are methods of analysis which can not be felicitously applied to the novel unless the mutations and transformations of mythical paradigms are also considered.

[42] ALISON WEBER: «Cuatro clases de narrativa picaresca», in *La Picaresca: Orígenes, Textos y Estructuras,* ed. Manuel Criado de Val (Madrid: Fundación Universitaria Española, 1979), pp. 13-18. Weber's notion of the picaresque genre is structural, conceived of as a system of semantic possibilities; whereas Guillén's is historical and rooted in the actual works.

[43] BAKHTIN: *Problems of Dostoevsky's Poetics,* p. 160.

original work, to expose as false some of its moral, philosophical, or aesthetic assumptions, and even to undermine its *Weltanschauung*. In those respects, the purpose of parody may be negative—to ridicule and point out the contradictions or insufficiencies of something. Yet this critical stance can be regarded as the beginning of a dialogue or a point of departure. One often parodies that which is impossible to suffer, condone, or believe in—that which one wishes to distance from oneself. Thus parody records the beginnings of liminality, of non-belonging, of an in-between stage when things are not what they were nor have yet become what they will be. We momentarily inhabit a never-never land of negativity that is magical because it lies at the interstices of experience and value systems. Parody is heuristic, self-conscious, playful, and critical. Yet parody is written to amuse and may display an affectionate attitude toward its subject, now better understood.

The polemical nature of the picaresque genre and the prevalence of negative intertextual relationships among the works have some important implications for the reader and the roles designed for him by the author. The primary purpose of rhetoric —the art of persuasion— is evident in the narrative devices of the novels. Each writer in his own individual style attempts to persuade the reader of the truth of his version of picaresque life in contrast to that of the «competition». The rhetoric of picaresque fiction is influenced both by deference to the reader and the remembrance of other texts. Writers go to considerable lengths to shape the reader's beliefs and to direct his understanding of the significance of the narration. I do not wish to imply that the reader is dictated to, or to oversimplify what is a complex process. Through various narrative techniques, picaresque fiction often presents the reader with choices or alternative perspectives on events. Some writers, to say the least, seemingly protect themselves by catering to readers of differing views. Thus their approach to the reader is somewhat devious or subtle, and is often reflected in the image or images of the hypothetical reader. The picaresque novel presents the reader with empirical reality, both commonplace and extraordinary experience, which he must visualize in his own mind. The building of these illusions demands the active participation of the reader, and the resulting interiorization of the unsettling world of the fiction involves the reader in the search for potential solutions. The picaresque novel demands a high degree of reader participation because it is polemical, realistic, and problematical. The semantic structures of the picaresque depend on the relationship established between narrator, reader, and the system of values represented in the fictitious world.

The Pleasure of the Picaresque: The Tragic, Comic, and Ironic Modes

It seems clear that the *pícaro* captured the interest of the Renaissance and post-Renaissance reader because of his novelty and controversial nature. To the twentieth-century reader he is perhaps all too familiar a figure in both literature and life—his motives and quandaries endemic yet without resolution. In both instances the reader is induced to clarify his attitudes

31

toward the *pícaro* and society, and his interpretation is dependent on those assessments. It is widely accepted that one reads imaginative literature for entertainment or pleasure, whether or not one accepts a Freudian interpretation of the function of art in the individual psyche—to return us «to the sources of pleasure that have been rendered inaccessible by the capitulation to the reality principle which we call education or maturity.» [44] One is then prompted to question just what is the «pleasure» of the picaresque and whether the effect is the same or different for readers of the past and readers of the present. Surely the *pícaro* is an uncomfortable and ambiguous character, «worse than ourselves,» sometimes comic (but not maintaining his proper distance), sometimes tragic, yet at times inspiring repugnance as well as pity and fear—a figure who threatens the social order and introduces doubts about the reader's relationship to that order. Does the picaresque give pleasure because of its linguistic playfulness and humor, an alchemy which transforms the *pícaro*'s pain to the reader's pleasure? [45] Or might we classify it in terms of Barthes' «text of bliss» as one that «breaks with culture», a «text that imposes a state of loss, that discomforts (perhaps to the point of a certain boredom), unsettles the reader's historical, cultural, psychological assumptions, the consistency of his tastes, values, memories, and finally brings to a crisis his relation with language? [46] Or does the *pícaro* evoke in the reader a response akin to that of the tragic hero? Aristotle based his definition of tragedy partly on its effect, the arousal of pity and fear in the audience, and he categorized character relative to the spectator—as better than, same as, or worse than ourselves. Yet it would seem impossible to define the picaresque similarly according to reader response, due to the many differences between individual *pícaros* and the varied reaction to them from one historical period to another, and from one reader to another. For example, many early readers must have interpreted *Lazarillo* and *El Buscón* as comic, and certainly both works are more easily comprehended within the context of Renaissance comedy. Like *Gargantua et Pantagruel* and the *Quijote,* they are both comic and serious in nature, works of profound comedy that place great demands on the reader's interpretive powers. In these works the comic cannot be associated with the frivolous or unimportant, or with the return to a socially stable order or *status quo,* such as is often exemplified by a wedding in a drawing-room comedy. Renaissance comic works are more ambiguous and more unsettling. The question of reader response becomes important (though puzzling and complex in explaining the significance of these particular works) and should help to explain the nature

[44] NORMAN O. BROWN: *Life Against Death* (New York: Vintage Books, 1959), p. 60.

[45] Such a view of the effect of *Lazarillo* is suggested in GEORGE SHIPLEY's «Making the Case against Lázaro de Tormes», *PMLA,* 97 (March, 1982), p. 191.

[46] ROLAND BARTHES: *The Pleasure of the Text,* trans. Richard Miller (New York: Hill and Wang, 1975), p. 14. Barthes' idea of a «text of bliss» seems similar to Fish's notion of dialectical presentation, although Barthes stresses the pleasure of rebelling against reigning ideologies and therapeutic release. On Barthes' notion of pleasure, see FRANK LENTRICCHIA: *After the New Criticism* (Chicago: University of Chicago Press, 1980), pp. 141-145.

of the *pícaro* as a comic character. In this regard a consideration of carnivalesque structures and their significance for picaresque narrative and
reader interpretation may also be enlightening.

Earlier in this chapter (pp. 21-22) I compared the relationships established between hero and reader in epic and romance with the relationship of
the picaresque anti-hero and the reader. In the former genres the hero is ad-
mirable and worthy of imitation, and his exemplariness and the narration's
meaning are more or less imposed on the accepting reader. In «non-heroic
mimesis», on the other hand, the reader is presented with a protagonist
whose life is neither enviable nor worthy of emulation.[47] The production of
meaning ultimately depends on the reader, for he must develop an attitude
toward the character and the social norms depicted in the novel. His
attitude toward the fiction will be partly determined by his own political
persuasions and judgment of the truthfulness of the narrative material. In
this respect, and for all the author's attempted control of response, the
picaresque may call forth differing reactions on the part of different readers.
In a recent article (and basing her judgment on Northrup Frye's theory of
narrative modes), Alison Weber suggests that there resides a modal polarity
in picaresque narrative between the comic, in which the norms of society
are ultimately upheld, and the ironic, in which society is judged to be
corrupt.[48] The former leads to social integration, the latter to social disintegration. A second polarity is to be found in the presentation of the
general and static as opposed to the particular and dynamic. Picaresque
fiction may be presented as a story —an example of the universal and
typical, or as a novel— the imitation of the specific, individual, and historical. Each class —ironic novel, ironic story, comic novel, and comic
story— makes possible a different relationship between reader, protagonist,
and social norm. The novel is dynamic and the reader's relationship with
the protagonist may change as the novel progresses. In the ironic novel the
reader realizes the incompatibility between positive values and the social
norms that are represented. The reader's original repugnance toward the
protagonist's antisocial values may turn to sympathy if he agrees with the
pícaro's negative vision. Then success within the societal system is less
admired than is failure. At the end of the comic novel, on the other hand,
there is resolution and agreement between the reader, the protagonist, and
society.

Whereas in the novel the protagonist's adventures involve a quest for
and the framing of values, the ironic story presents a clash between a
degrading but static society and an imposter or trickster. The result is the
unmasking or devaluing of the social norm. In the comic story the *pícaro*
is an eccentric who attacks the system that the reader upholds. He is distanced and laughed at and ultimately punished.

In all of the above instances, which should not be regarded as mutually
exclusive categories, the semantic structure of the narration depends on
the reader's reaction to the narrative material. The author uses many tech-

---

[47] Cf. HANS ROBERT JAUSS: «Levels of Identification of Hero and Audience»,
New Literary History, V (Winter, 1974), 283-317.
[48] WEBER: «Cuatro clases de narrativa picaresca», 13-18.

niques to attempt to manipulate that reaction, and at the same time displays an awareness of the differences in readers. Much of the meaning of the picaresque work in question depends on its tone or mode which, within the realm of possibilities discussed here, may shift and change. Furthermore, the author's attitude toward the *pícaro* and society is transmitted to the reader through the reader's own perceptions and preconceptions. Because of such ambiguities many picaresque works (and in particular those under consideration here) have been subjected to a wide variety of interpretations.

The Act of Reading, and the Interpretation of the Picaresque

The narrative devices utilized in the picaresque in regard to the reader are particularly interesting not only because the *pícaro* is controversial, but also because picaresque works are at the crossroads between oral and written narrative. It is evident that a narrative must please its audience or readership if it is to be listened to or read. But in the transition from oral to written narrative,[49] the function of the listener, now the absent reader, appreciably changed.[50] Works of fiction written at the time when reading was evolving into a fundamentally private experience often simulate through various narrative techniques the conditions of oral narrative.

The skillful teller of tales improvises in response to his audience's reactions and alters, ornaments, reduces, or amplifies traditional material. The teller of tales presents the skeleton of a story, more or less fleshed out, which the listener may further embellish. The listener builds images of the events and characters of the story in his mind's eye. The listener may influence the development of the tale by indicating his pleasure or impatience to the narrator, but he must closely follow the narrator's lead. The reader, on the other hand, enjoys a far greater freedom than the listener in that he can control the pace at which he assimilates the work and depart from the text without losing what is to follow. However, the writer does not have the advantage of directly experiencing the reader's reactions while he is in the process of fabricating his fiction. He can only imagine a reader, and how he might react, and must mold his tale accordingly. Thus the demands on the writer are more constricting, and the reader exercises a greater range of choice than does the audience or listener in the way he reads and interprets. Many early works of fiction, destined to be printed and distributed to a growing reading public, attempt to compensate for the lost advantages of oral narrative by presenting fictional audiences or listeners within the texts. Their fictional responses to the narration invite the real readers to consider the stance indicated, or to fictionalize themselves in regard to the text in the way the author deems appropriate. All

---

[49] Cf. INÉS AZAR: «Meaning, Intention, and the Written Text: Anthony Close's Approach to Don Quijote and its Critics», *MLN*, 96, no. 2 (March, 1981), p. 444; and BARBARA HERNSTEIN SMITH: *On the Margins of Discourse* (Chicago: University of Chicago Press, 1978).
[50] ISER: *The Act of Reading*, pp. 108-112.

the texts examined in this study, and particularly *Lazarillo*, are written texts that often seem spoken and contain many reminiscences from the oral tradition.

But there are also many similarities in the way that oral and written narrative are experienced. Both reading and listening are dynamic processes, and the narrative work is apprehended sequentially and not initially or abruptly as a painting or sculpture might be. Rather, the text gradually unfolds. The literary work is thus a different sort of aesthetic entity than a work of art perceived visually, because the initial effect of a narrative is necessarily sequential, a happening that takes place in time and cannot be comprehended at a glance. The characters and action of the narration are visualized or imagined by the reader. The work of fiction offers him an incomplete schematization which he must complement with his repertoire of values, life experience, and ideas in order to form a picture of the characters and events in his own mind. The reader actively participates in rendering the text intelligible to himself. He must fill in the gaps and constuct a comprehensive totality. Interpretation continues after the book is closed, whereupon the significance of the text takes effect in and works upon the reader's own existence as he relates it to his experience, knowledge of other literary works, philosophical ideas, or religious beliefs. Thus the dichotomy that Todorov insists upon—reading as both an «intratextual» and «intertextual» experience —or Northrup Frye's two processes of reading— the centripetal or inward, and the centrifugal or outward.[51]

Because of the nature of the act of reading, no theoretical discussion can do justice to the vast differences in individual readings and readers. How one interprets is a unique and private matter. As Barthes remarked in *Le Plaisir du Texte*, there are the «grazers» and the «gobblers», as well as those who alternate between grazing and globbling and do so inconsistently. Barthes himself claims never to have read Proust in the same way twice; that is, he slowly savoured certain passages and skimmed others quickly—and never the same passages.[52] Thus, no two readers and no two readings are ever exactly alike.

Since reading is a highly subjective activity, I shall only speculate on those essential differences between contemporary and twentieth-century interpretations that dispel a myopic vision of the genre. Literature is a social institution, and the cultural background of a community of readers will necessarily bear on their perception of a literary work. Therefore, a viable means of analysis must take into account both the work's proper historical context and the reader's horizon of expectation.[53]

[51] NORTHRUP FRYE: *Anatomy of Criticism. Four Essays* (Princeton: Princeton University Press, 1973), p. 73.

[52] BARTHES: *The Pleasure of the Text*, p. 13.

[53] JAUSS suggests that literary history should be based on a history of reader response. See, for example, «Literary History as a Challenge to Literary Theory», *New Literary History*, II, no. 1 (1970-1971), 7-31.

CHAPTER II

COMEDY, IRONY, AND THE READER
IN *LA VIDA DE LAZARILLO DE TORMES*

Introduction

There is no doubt that *Lazarillo* is a work that has inspired widely
diverse interpretations, but the reasons for this ambiguity are not clear.
Why has *Lazarillo* been read as cynical or comic or even as both? In the
latter two cases, what is the nature of the humor? If it is conceived in the
spirit of Renaissance carnivalesque humor, does it invite the reader's participation, catharsis, and a return to normalcy? Or is the work written as
a protest, and is it accordingly sarcastic and subversive? Is the intent of
Lazarillo like that of the Feast of Fools, wherein the reverse of the usual
is celebrated for a day, or is the message here more bitter, tinged with
resentment, and critical of both contemporary mores and the absurd
idealism of chivalric literature? Finally, is there a difference in the way
that sixteenth and twentieth-century readers interpret the work due to
their differing expectations in regard to fiction?

It is my contention that a study of the image and role of the reader
indicated within the text is a point of departure for providing some of the
answers to these questions. In this chapter I shall discuss the author's
approach to the reader in the prologue and text with particular emphasis
on the function of the fictional reader, Vuestra Merced. Vuestra Merced
and other fictional *destinataires* in *Lazarillo* function like filters through
which the author both guides and varies the real reader's response to his
work. In effect, the elusive author of *Lazarillo* presents the reader with
a series of lenses through which to view his narrative, and provides an
ever shifting perspective on events or at least many alternative ways of
seeing things. Other characteristics of the text induce the reader to identify
with the fictional characters and situations and to vicariously relive the
narration, but the differing cultural experience of sixteenth and twentieth-
century readers necessarily affects their understanding of the work. The
possible relationships established between reader, protagonist, and society,
and the very tone and texture of the tale become more clearly defined in
the context of these considerations, the many readers and readings of *Lazarillo* notwithstanding.

The Prologue of «Lazarillo»

Not surprisingly, the prologue of *Lazarillo* offers specific indications as to the type of reader the author is addressing and how the work should be read. I believe that the first portion of the prologue (up to «y todo va desta manera») is written in the form of a direct address from the author to his readers, and that the guise of pseudo-autobiography is assumed in the middle of the prologue and thereafter never abandoned.[1] The only exceptions to this rule are the headings at the beginning of each *tratado*, written in the third person and generally indicating the profession of Lazarillo's next master; for example, «Como Lázaro se asentó con un clérigo y de las cosas que con él pasó.» They emphasize the succession of different masters that Lazarillo endures and thus the basic structure of the narration. The title of the first *tratado*, «Cuenta Lázaro su vida y cuyo hijo fue,» may be the most significant because his origins largely determine what follows.[2] Lazarillo owes his formation and education not only to his parents, but also to Zaide and more especially to the blindman, whom he regards as his spiritual father («... después de Dios, éste [el ciego] me dio la vida»).[3] Lazarillo is the child of these early influences, an interpretation substantiated by his behavior in various episodes, the circular structure of the narrative, and its ending.

The prologue is replete with difficulties and paradoxes. Nonetheless it functions as a port of entry and orientation to the narration. Considerable space is devoted to explaining the importance of a desire for honor as inspiration and sustainer of the arts, a somewhat puzzling emphasis due to the anonymity of the author and the social insignificance of the protagonist. The idea seems to be that the *book itself* must become famous and will do so by attracting many readers. The epic-like beginning,[4] «Yo por bien tengo que cosas tan señaladas, y por ventura nunca oídas ni vistas, vengan a noticias de muchos y no se entierran en la sepultura de olvido,» in the light of the humble class and non-heroic demeanor of the protagonist, may be understood as parodic. The novel ends on a similarly ironic note when Lazarillo's «prosperity» and «good fortune» are juxtaposed to the glorious victories of the Spanish Empire. At the same time, on another level, the insignificant life of Lazarillo acquires significance in the course of the narration, and in this sense the beginning of the prologue may also be taken at face value.[5]

[1] A. Bell: «The Rhetoric of Self Defence of Lázaro de Tormes», *MLR*, 68 (1973), 84-93.

[2] Douglas M. Carey: «Lazarillo de Tormes and the Quest for Authority», *PMLA*, 94 (1979), 36-46.

[3] *La Vida de Lazarillo de Tormes*, ed. Alberto Blecua (Madrid: Clásicos Castalia, 1972), p. 97. All quotes will be taken from this edition and the page numbers will be cited in the text itself.

[4] Ernest Robert Curtius: *European Literature and the Latin Middle Ages* (1963, rpt. Princeton: Princeton University Press, 1973), pp. 85-89.

[5] Harry Sieber's important *Language and Society in La Vida de Lazarillo de Tormes* (Baltimore and London: Johns Hopkins University Press, 1978) discusses Lazarillo's creation of self and reality through the act of writing.

The author grants the reader a life-bestowing role in regard to his book which, unless read, «will be buried in the tomb of forgetfulness.» Later in the prologue he emphasizes that he hopes his book will be favorably received by many readers, and demonstrates that this desire for fame or honor is not peculiar to writers, but motivates diverse endeavors. He quotes Cicero, «la honra cría las artes,» [6] and states that honor not only inspires artists, but also the soldier going into battle and the novice priest preparing to preach. The author reminds the reader that he, too, likes to be admired, «mas preguntan a su merced si le pesa cuando le dicen: 'Oh que maravillosamente lo ha hecho vuestra reverencia!'» (p. 88). Thus the reader is implicated in the author's view of human nature, and the desire for admiration universalized. The reader, the writer, the soldier, the prelate, and the novel's protagonist, Lazarillo, are all similarly motivated and covet praise («todo va desta manera»). The author implies that even undeserved honor is solicited and enjoyed, a theme often illustrated in the course of the narration by the appearance of numerous imposters. A good reputation is so important to man that he rewards the lying flatterer: «Justó muy ruinmente el señor don Fulano y dio el saÿete de armas al truán porque lo loaba de haber llevado muy buenas lanzas. ¿Qué hiciera si fuera verdad?» (p. 89). The author sustains a view of human nature in which man tries to appear better than he is in the eyes of others.

Understandably, therefore, the writer addresses himself to many readers in hopes of their praise: «Muy pocos escribirían para uno solo, pues no se hace sin trabajo, y quieren, ya que lo pasan, ser recompensados no con dineros, mas con que vean y lean sus obras, y, si hay de qué, se las alaben» (p. 88). The work is repeatedly directed to many readers and not just to a select few. The author hoped his fiction would reach, it would seem, the general reading public of the time and merit their approval.

Yet in an earlier passage the author had expressed doubts about how his book would be received and whether readers would find it appealing. His ironic approach to the social insignificance of Lazarillo, indirectly compared to soldiers, priests, emperors, and epic heroes, is indicative of an ambivalent attitude either toward his own protagonist or toward society. The fact that the author remains anonymous suggests he may be fearful about the work's reception or his own safety; like the soldier he mentions, he is undertaking something dangerous in hopes of praise: «Mas el deseo de alabanza le hace ponerse al peligro» (p. 88). Both the elusiveness of the author's voice throughout the remainder of the text and the ambiguity of the work support this view. Also, the author seems to anticipate an adverse reaction on the part of some readers and, quoting Pliny and Horace, asks the reader's indulgence and tolerance:

---

[6] FRANCISCO RICO in Introducción a *La Novela Picaresca Española* (Barcelona: Planeta, 1967), p. LII, suggests that «la honra cría las artes» may be understood in retrospect to have a double meaning, since the motive of the book is to explain the *caso* and the *caso* is a «caso de honra». Lazarillo's bad reputation provides the fictional *raison d'être* of the work.

... no hay libro por malo que sea que no tenga alguna cosa buena. Mayormente que los gustos no son todos unos, mas lo que uno no come, otro se pierde por ello; y así vemos cosas tenidas en poco de algunas, que de otros no lo son. Y esto, para que ninguna cosa debría romper ni echar a mal, si muy detestable no fuese, sino que a todos se comunicase, mayormente siendo sin perjuicio y pudiendo sacar della algún fructo. (p. 88)

The disproportionate length of and precedence given to these commonplaces indicate the author's fear that his book may offend. Thus the passage functions as an apologetic defense of the work's value and a coy justification for its very existence: even a bad work should not be destroyed because it may please someone who will «sacar della algún fructo,» a traditional phrase usually referring to the moral lesson that a reader will derive from the narrative material.

However, mention of the dual role of literature, to please and teach («deleitar y enseñar»), so axiomatic to medieval and Renaissance hermeneutics, is conspicuous by its absence earlier on in the text. This omission is to my mind the most innovative feature of the prologue and represents a departure from the writer's conventional advice to readers. The author of *Lazarillo* seems to asume a new epistemological orientation toward the reader, and to expect an aesthetic response to his work at variance with traditional interpretation. «Pues podría ser que alguno que las lea, halle algo que le *agrade,* y a los que no ahondaren tanto, los *deleite*» (p. 87). As Stephen Gilman has pointed out, «agrade» is substituted for the expected «aproveche,» [7] thus giving equal value to a surface and a deeper reading. Those who fathom the surface may expect the same reward as those who merely skim—pleasure. No mention is made of the discovery of a moral. Perhaps, as Fred Abrams points out, «the author is addressing himself to two types of readers, those who are interested in reading purely for enjoyment and those who wish to penetrate more deeply to catch the satirical message the text holds specifically for them.» [8] Both deep and surface readings give pleasure, and this is the «fruit» that a reader can be expected to extract from a work. Appearances are no longer the veil that conceals meaning; rather the author is bringing to the world something that did not exist before, «cosas nunca oídas ni vistas,» for the reader to consider. The relationship between fiction and value, or fiction and didactic and philosophical content in *Lazarillo* differs from most medieval works. Yet the author suggests in no uncertain terms that both a deep and surface reading of the work are possible. How these readings may differ is a subject to which I shall return at the end of the chapter.

In the first portion of the prologue the implied author posits some general truths about the motivation for writing, indicates to whom the present work is addressed, and advises the reader as to how the work should be

---

[7] STEPHEN GILMAN: «The Death of Lazarillo de Tormes», *PMLA*, 81 (1966), 149; cf. M. J. WOODS: «Pitfalls for the Moralizer in *Lazarillo de Tormes*», *MLR*, LXXIV (1979), 595; RICO: «Introducción», p. LXVI.

[8] FRED ABRAMS: «To Whom was the Anonymous *Lazarillo de Tormes* dedicated?», *Romance Notes*, 8 (1966), p. 273.

approached. In the second half of the prologue, the fictional narrator, Lazarillo, describes the fictional *raison d'être* of the work. The transition from the author's voice to that of the narrator is not explicit, but may be surmised from the narrator's characterization of himself as no more saintly than his neighbors and his admission that he has written a «nonada», i.e., an insignificant piece, in vulgar style, qualities more easily identified with Lazarillo than with the learned humanist author. Like the aforementioned soldier, writer, and prelate, Lazarillo would be pleased if his work were to please someone. He also wants his readers to know that there lives a man with so many «fortunas, peligros, y adversidades.» The implication is that the reader stands to be amazed by his life story, but not necessarily instructed. It can be deduced that Lazarillo, being no more saintly than his neighbors, also desires praise (as does the reader). Again a leveling is implied; Lazarillo, his neighbors, and the reader are similarly vulnerable.

Hereupon a fictional reader and a situational pretext for the work's existence are introduced. The work is addressed to a «Vuestra Merced,» who has instructed Lazarillo to write to him and to explain «el caso». «Y pues Vuestra Meced escribe se le escriba y relate el caso muy por extenso.» In answer to Vuestra Merced's request, Lazarillo writes a detailed account of his life from its very beginning. The phrase «relate el caso» suggests that Lazarillo's life is not simply told as a letter, but as the sort of letter that functions as a «legal deposition» or prelude to a petition to a higher authority. According to González Echevarría, the form of the picaresque developed by imitating «one of the formulas of forensic rhetoric much in use at the time: the *relación*.» Legal and quasi-legal documents in search of acquittal or advancement were extremely common in the Sixteenth Century, particularly among the *crónicas de la conquista*. Furthermore, the word «caso» not only has a common generalized meaning —case, matter, or scandal— but also a more specific legal one. According to Covarrubias, «it is equivalent to an event that has occurred; thus lawyers call *caso* the issue or proposition on which the legal determination is based; and in legal actions the first thing on which they must agree is the case or fact, which is all one and the same.»[9] Future literary *pícaros*, such as Guzmán de Alfarache and Ginés de Pasamonte, were in trouble with the law, corroborating the view that the original picaresque text, *Lazarillo*, is directed to someone in authority—perhaps even a judge or ecclesiastical official. Lazarillo's account is a confession and a self-justification addressed to a paternal figure in power over him. In the final *tratado* we finally learn that Lazarillo actively curries favor with the mighty. He is still awaiting some benefit from the Archpriest and friend of Vuestra Merced. «... mi señor me ha prometido lo que pienso cumplirá» (p. 175). The *pícaro* writes as a suppliant aware of his humble position and dependence on the rich and powerful.

Lazarillo's other stated reason for telling his life story is directed to

---

[9] ROBERTO GONZÁLEZ ECHEVARRÍA: «The Life and Adventures of Cipión: Cervantes and the Picaresque», *Diacritics* (Sept. 1980), 18-21; COVARRUBIAS is quoted on p. 20.

some hypothetical readers, rather than a fictional reader within the text. «... y también porque consideren los que heredaron nobles estados cuán poco se les debe, pues fortuna fue con ellos parcial, y cuánto más hicieron los que, siéndoles contraria, con fuerza y maña remando salieron a buen puerto» (p. 89). Here Lazarillo is directing himself to the nobility or to those who have inherited wealth. He posits a contrast between their undeservedly easy existence and his own precarious struggle. Note that he first addresses himself to his fictional reader, Vuestra Merced, and then to a wider group of readers, «los que heredaron nobles estados,» nonetheless a more select group than the entire readership of his work and singled out to be humbled. Their unfavorable contrast with the actively ambitious might give pleasure to another group of readers, those who have not inherited noble estates.

By the end of the prologue, the state of knowledge of Lazarillo, the hypothetical reader(s), and the fictional reader (Vuestra Merced) varies. Vuestra Merced clearly knows something about the *caso,* though the hypothetical reader does not; Vuestra Merced knows more than this reader, but not as much as he should like. Lazarillo implies that he has succeeded in life, that he is one who was not born to wealth, but through effort and cleverness has ended up well. In retrospect that assessment will probably seem ironic to the reader and no doubt already does to Vuestra Merced. Vuestra Merced refers to the «caso» and Lazarillo to those who «remando salieron a buen puerto.» The irony lies in the difference in their point of view and motivation; Vuestra Merced is curious about the *caso,* whereas Lazarillo is anxious to prove that he has been successful in life.

In addressing both Vuestra Merced and «los que heredaron nobles estados,» Lazarillo is directing his narration to readers of superior social status. His approach to Vuestra Merced is initially respectful, polite, and even obsequious. «Suplico a Vuestra Merced reciba el pobre servicio de mano de quien lo hiciera más rico, si su poder y deseo se conformaran.» At the end of the passage, however, he issues a challenge to a whole class of readers. This variation in attitude is a quite constant feature of Lazarillo. A conciliatory or fawning statement is followed by a truism in the form of a challenge to the reader or an attack on the value system or social mores of sixteenth-century Spain, here quite boldly presented to the aristocratic reader. Later in the narration Lazarillo more often than not states these criticisms to himself in the form of an aside «overheard» by the reader, but not by any fictional character involved in the action of the narration. Only the reader and the fictional reader, Vuestra Merced, are privy to Lazarillo's private thoughts as he recalls them in the process of narrating his tale.

«Vuestra Merced»: His function in the Narration and Relationship to the Real Reader

It is difficult to specify how the real reader should relate to Vuestra Merced. His character and identity are, after all, extremely vague. We can surmise from the final chapter that he is a friend of the Archpriest with whom Lazarillo shares his wife, from the prologue that he is curious to learn more about the *caso,* and from Lazarillo's deferential attitude toward him in the course of the narration that he is superior in social status to Lazarillo. One purpose in including Vuestra Merced as fictitious reader is to introduce to the real reader a possible perspective or standpoint from which to view the events of the narration. The stance indicated may be described as that of a curious listener of superior social status, qualifications easily satisfied by most of Lazarillo's contemporary readership. Vuestra Merced is always there listening (or reading) from a position of power or authority. Lazarillo mentions him by name periodically throughout the narration, and one may assume that at those times the author wished to remind us of his presence. But Vuestra Merced not only indicates a role for the reader in viewing events, but also serves as a reminder that the reader is *outside* the events, witness to a dialogue between Lazarillo and Vuestra Merced. To some extent, therefore, Vuestra Merced is useful as a distancing device, and the reader then assumes the role of an eavesdropper. At other times Vuestra Merced's presence colors the narrative, for Lazarillo often assumes a deferential and apologetic attitude when reminded of his authority. Lazarillo might have told a somewhat different tale, were he explaining his life to his mother, a group of *pícaros* at a wayside inn, or his wife. Vuestra Merced also provides the pretext for his telling the tale in the first place, since Lazarillo is writing to explain the *caso.*

In *Lazarillo,* the determining influence of the fictional *destinataire,* Vuestra Merced, is significant because, through his presence, the effect of the reader's anticipated response weighs heavily on the development of the narrative. *Lazarillo* is an example of a text that evolves in imaginary dialogue with its readership, giving credence to the remarks of Bakhtin and Kristeva (see pp. 25 ff.). Moreover, this inclusion of a *destinataire* within a work of art is a technique by no means confined to prose fiction; an analogous configuration often occurs in Renaissance painting. Medieval and especially Renaissance artists frequently portrayed their patrons in paintings devoted to other subjects, a constant reminder of the painter's economic dependence on his patron and, conversely, the patron's influence on his art. Both the painter and writer must please the appropriate people if their work is to survive. The patrons portrayed are not fictional, yet they function within the painting in a similar way to Vuestra Merced in *Lazarillo.*

A case in point is Velázquez's painting of «Las Meninas»:[10] the resemblance between the presence of a fictitious reader in *Lazarillo* and the mirror image of the King and Queen in the back of Velázquez's painting. The Royal Couple are portrayed as observers who intervene by implication in the viewer's perception of the scene, since they all occupy the same space outside the painting. Should the spectator identify with the royal couple themselves or only with their viewpoint? In a sense, the painting is hermetic in that it contains its own most important spectators. Those who

[10] For a very subtle, more complete, and quite different discussion of «Las Meninas», see MICHEL FOUCAULT: *The Order of Things,* trans. *Les Mots et les Choses,* ed. R. D. Laing (New York: Vintage Books), pp. 3-16.

follow are but an afterthought—intruders in a scene already graced by the presence of royalty.

The painter's or author's use of a fictitious spectator or reader indicates to the real spectator or reader possible ways in which he may relate to the painting or text. The work of art's existence and particular configuration appear to depend on a mandate from an important person or persons—in the case of *Lazarillo,* Vuestra Merced, and in «Las Meninas», the King and Queen. The reader or viewer may regard the work from their vantage point, putting himself in their shoes so to speak, or he may consider himself an outsider who is offered an opportunity to witness a private encounter, the interruption of a princess's portrait being painted or an explanatory letter requested by Vuestra Merced. The reader and spectator are presented with ambiguous or even contradictory directions, invited to participate in the text or painting through a possibly uncomfortable identification with Vuestra Merced or the King and Queen, yet reminded that their presence is an afterthought. The Royal Couple's presence dominates the moment and makes the painting happen in the way that it happens. Eyes focus on them as other activities are suspended. Likewise, Vuestra Merced's request makes possible Lazarillo's tale and determines the form in which it is told. Yet *Lazarillo*'s author has explicitly expressed a desire for many readers and implied that the work cannot live without being read. The introduction of a fictional reader or observer, then, is something of a ruse or fictional device through which the author or painter is able to guide the reader's response to his work and enable him to perceive it in more than one way. Thus the reader enjoys a shifting perspective from which to view Lazarillo's life, now from the vantage point of Vuestra Merced, now from some other place.

A word should perhaps be said about what is commonly called the identification of the reader with what he reads, or with characters he finds sympathetic or like himself. This establishment of similarities between reader or his experience and someone or something outside himself no doubt enables him to comprehend the narrative material and to relive the narrative in his own imagination. The reader in this respect is not confined to one role, but may «identify» in one way or another with various characters and situations. The author uses various stratagems to «establish a familiar ground on which we are able to experience the unfamiliar,» [11] and the introduction of a fictitious reader assumed to be like the intended reader is one such narrative technique. But it is by no means the only one. Most readers readily identify with a sympathetic protagonist, such as Lazarillo. As Georges Poulet suggests, when one reads one mentally pronounces an «I», and yet the «I» one pronounces is not oneself. Reading in a sense introduces a division into the reader himself. While reading he is both himself and an alien self or selves. Thus fiction may induce the reader to experience vicariously several new modes of being which, through

[11] ISER: *The Implied Reader,* p. 291.

the dialectical process of reading, contribute to defining his own desires and values.[12]

Because of the epistolary structure of *Lazarillo,* Vuestra Merced's shadowy presence is a given constant throughout the narration. The situations in which Lazarillo addresses him directly are significant, although their function in guiding reader response seems to vary. Lazarillo most often mentions Vuestra Merced in the first and final *tratados.* He directs himself to Vuestra Merced only once in the third *tratado* and not at all in *tratados* II, IV, V, and VI, at least in the editions of Amberes and Burgos.[13] In the first *tratado* Lazarillo emphasizes certain facts which are important for Vuestra Merced to understand by periodically addressing him directly. He stresses who his parents are and that his harsh childhood demonstrates the truth of the message of the prologue—that it is difficult to rise in society when one is humbly born. Indeed his purpose in recounting his childhood is made explicit. «Huelgo de contar a Vuestra Merced estas niñerías para mostrar cuánta virtud sea saber los hombres subir siendo bajos y dejarse bajar siendo altos cuánto vicio» (p. 97). Lazarillo directly addresses Vuestra Merced three times when explaining or exemplifying to him the evil and crafty character of the blindman. This stress given to the blindman's character is important because of his influence on Lazarillo's education and spiritual formation. Later when the blindman prophesies that Lazarillo will be fortunate with wine, Lazarillo verifies to Vuestra Merced the future truth of the prophecy: «lo que aquel día me dijo salirme tan verdadero como adelante Vuestra Merced oirá» (p. 110). The paths which Lazarillo's future life and psychological development will follow are indicated, then, in the first *tratado,* and Lazarillo draws Vuestra Merced's attention to the blindman's culpability and his own innocence and suffering.

Vuestra Merced is addressed once in the third *tratado,* again when Lazarillo is considering the theme of fortune, bemoaning his fate. He has just discovered the poverty and hunger of his third master and experiences a moment of reflection in which he realizes that the downward spiral of his luck is more devastating to him than is hunger. «Vuestra Merced crea cuando esto le oí que estuve a punto de caer de mi estado, no tanto de hambre como por conoscer de todo en todo la fortuna serme adversa» (p. 132). Finally in the last *tratado* Vuestra Merced is mentioned for the purpose of supplying information to the reader about his identity and relationship to Lazarillo. Lazarillo is a *pregonero* of wines and in some way serves Vuestra Merced, who is presumably a resident of the same city or so Lazarillo implies: «vivo y resido a servicio de Dios y de Vuestra Merced» (p. 173). A little later, the Archpriest with whom Lazarillo shares his

[12] ISER: *The Implied Reader,* pp. 191-193, discusses GEORGES POULET's «Phenomenology of Reading», *New Literary History I* (1969), 54-59. PAUL DE MAN, in «Autobiography as Defacement», *MLN,* 94 (1979), 919-930, defines autobiography as a figure of reading or understanding, rather than a genre, which occurs to some degree in all texts when the reader and narrator are momentarily aligned (p. 921).

[13] In the edition of Alcalá there are frequent additions, presumably apocryphal, which I am not considering in my discussion. See BLECUA: *op, cit.,* pp. 7 and 57, n. 97.

wife is identified as a friend of Vuestra Merced, «servidor ȳ amigo de Vuestra Merced» (p. 173). As Francisco Rico has so effectively explained, the vague links between Lazarillo's final situation and Vuestra Merced, considered with Vuestra Merced's initial request to hear about the *caso,* give a circular structure to the narration,[14] the whole of which has explained the *caso,* the product of the narrative process. In the final paragraph Vuestra Merced is reminded that Charles the Fifth's glorious entry into Toledo took place the same year Lazarillo found himself at the peak of his good fortune. «Pues en este tiempo estaba en mi prosperidad y en la cumbre de toda buena fortuna» (p. 177). In conclusion, it seems evident that Vuestra Merced's attention is particularly drawn to the evil adults responsible for Lazarillo's formation, his changeable fortunes (or more often misfortunes), the difficulty with which someone not well-born rises in society, and the concluding episode of the *caso.* Both at the end of the prologue and at the end of the narration Vuestra Merced's curiosity about the *caso* is juxtaposed to Lazarillo's assessment of his now fortunate situation and success.

It has often been pointed out that the picaresque novel is a pseudo-autobiography and is narrated from a unitary point of view. In *Lazarillo,* the narrator is the *pícaro,* but the functional *destinataire* of his confidences changes frequently, providing the reader with a shifting perspective on events that accounts for much of the liveliness of the prose and irony of the narration. Lazarillo's experiences are refracted through various fictional listeners who offer differing responses to his tale, and he adjusts his discourse to their tastes or expectations. However, there are times when Lazarillo seems quite oblivious to the omnipresence of Vuestra Merced and utterly engrossed in the pleasure or poignancy of his own reminiscences. At other times he expresses the most cynical and heterodox insights about his fellow-man and the existing social order, as well as the value system on which it rested. Indeed, his life's experience leads him to express some rebellious and seditious opinions. Lazarillo's most malicious observations are usually stated as *apartes,* brief hostile comments made only to himself. His views have no effect on the course of events, but are a direct response to the way that he is treated and indicative of his inner development and the formation of his *Weltanschauung.* The bitterness of these remarks is countered by the polite hypocrisy of the various masks he presents to the world. Although the entire narration is directed to Vuestra Merced, the appropriateness and ingenuity of these *apartes* bring them swiftly home to the reader—like a shaft of light that suddenly illuminates, or arrows that fly to the mark. They stand out from the surface of the text because they are commentary, removed from the time sequence of the narrative. They record Lazarillo's immediate reaction to events when they occurred. Some readers may even interpret some or all of these *apartes* as authorial comments voiced through the persona of his fictional narrator. At the same time, they express Lazarillo's innermost and secret thoughts, and establish for him an intimate relationship with the reader.

Lazarillo's *apartes* generally distinguish between appearance and reality,

---

[14] Rico: *La Novela Picaresca y el punto de vista,* pp. 15-35.

and can be rather neatly divided into two complementary categories: the sarcastic aside unmasking an imposter or deceptive practice, and the reflective aside pondering some just-grasped truth about existence in a deceptive world.[15] Their distribution is similar to the direct addresses to Vuestra Merced in that they abound in the first three *tratados*. Unlike the addresses to Vuestra Merced, they are significantly absent in the final *tratado*, for here we are no longer privy to Lazarillo's private thoughts. Now, perhaps, he has joined the corrupt society from which he once stood apart.

There are thirteen *apartes* which are introduced by standard formulae (dixe passo, dixe entre mí, dezía yo passo entre mí): two in the first chapter, three in the second, seven in the third, and one in the fifth. Other comments made by Lazarillo may be interpreted as asides, but are longer and do not always deal with the world's deceptiveness, but with other themes as well.

In the first *tratado* Lazarillo is reflective in his asides and through his observations learns about human nature, develops self-awareness, and learns how to survive in a world of dissemblers. The first use of an aside occurs when Lazarillo's half-brother reacts with fear to his father's blackness, crying out «Madre, coco,» and Lazarillo remarks to himself («dije entre mí»): «Cuántos debe de haber en el mundo que huyen de otros porque no se veen a sí mismos» (p. 94). Man's inability to see himself as others see him is one common human weakness exemplified by this event and may cause the reader to ponder his own self-blindness. In both this and the subsequent *aparte* it is strongly implied that no man, rich or poor, is unique in his folly; for Lazarillo compares Zaide's thefts in order to support his beloved family to the less altruistic motivation of more illustrious thieves:

> No nos maravillemos de un clérigo ni fraile porque el uno hurta de los pobres, y el otro de casa para sus devotas y para ayuda de otro tanto, cuando a un pobre esclavo el amor le animaba a esto. (p. 94)

Thus Lazarillo, perhaps from the vantage point of his maturity, draws from his observations of individuals truisms about human frailty in general.

Lazarillo's next aside is delivered in response to the blindman's advice, «Necio, aprende que el mozo del ciego un punto ha de saber más que el diablo» (p. 96), after having knocked Lazarillo's head against the stone bull. Lazarillo is made aware of his essential aloneness and the necessity of defending himself in a world of tricksters. «Dije entre mí: 'Verdad dice éste, que me cumple avivar el ojo y avisar, pues solo soy, y pensar cómo me sepa valer'» (p. 96). The final *aparte* in the *tratado*, which I classify as such because no one overhears it, is addressed to the unconscious blindman over whom Lazarillo has finally triumphed: «Cómo, y olistes la longaniza y no el poste? Ole! Ole!» (p. 112). The blindman's unawareness of his victory constitutes a slight variation on the usual *burlador/burlado* situation, for Lazarillo is, significantly, rude only when no risk is involved.

Lazarillo's most aggressive and sarcastic asides are spoken in reaction

---

[15] Douglas M. Carey: «Asides and Interiority in *Lazarillo de Tormes*», *Studies in Philology*, XVI (1969), 131.

to his mistreatment by his first three masters.[16] He lashes out at them with his wit, exposing their greed or hypocrisy. The *escudero* provokes both sarcasm, tempered by pity, and reflection, for he is an impostor of a different sort. Here Lazarillo considers the absurdity of a value system that inspires a man to dissemble, yet still suffer hunger and material deprivation for the sake of a good reputation. Some of the digressions in the second and third *tratados* are not formulaic, are addressed to God or no one in particular, and are usually longer philosophical passages in which he discusses, for example, the brevity of pleasure and the longevity of bad fortune (p. 121), or the dreadful hardships suffered for the sake of honor by men such as the *escudero* (p. 137). These frank observations and interpretations of contemporary society offer a contrast to the apologetic tone often adopted when directly addressing Vuestra Merced. In *Lazarillo*, recall, the fitfully acknowledged presence of Vuestra Merced, life's experience, and the conjunction of stored wisdom and current strategy all bear upon the tone and texture of Lazarillo's tale. His attitude varies according to whom he addresses his remarks, or more to the point, he reveals various facets of his character to the appropriate *destinataire*.[17] In general, he is eager to please Vuestra Merced, cynical when musing to himself, and ruefully philosophical when directing his thoughts to God. The dichotomy between the inner critical man and the outwardly pragmatic man is thus indicated.

The real author, then, routes his narration to the real reader through a fictional narrator, Lazarillo, and a fictitious reader, Vuestra Merced, whose presence at times shapes the character of the narration and at times is apparently forgotten. Within this framework there are further intricacies, for Lazarillo, although ultimately telling his tale to Vuestra Merced, reports what he said or thought to himself or God. Lazarillo also recounts his interactions with the other fictional characters in the novel. These relationships are generally characterized by a great degree of deception and mistrust, and indirectly enhance the reader's sympathetic identification with Lazarillo.

Through Lazarillo's dialogues and relationships with other characters in the narration, the reader gains knowledge of how Lazarillo views the world and also how the world views Lazarillo. Lazarillo's various masters perceive him as a deceitful and lazy boy, as do most others. Society's attitude toward him is typified by the scene at the beginning of the third *tratado*. When Lazarillo appears bruised and battered from his encounter with the *clérigo* of Maqueda, people are willing to give him alms. But once he has recovered, he is expected to seek work, not live off charity. Then people say to him, «Tú bellaco y gallofero eres. Busca, busca un amo a quien sirvas» (p. 129).

---

[16] CAREY: «Asides and Interiority...», pp. 126-129.

[17] ANTONIO GÓMEZ-MORIANA, in «La subversión del discurso ritual; una lectura intertextual del *Lazarillo de Tormes*» (*Imprévue*, 1980-1981), p. 63, suggests that three conventional modes of autobiographical discourse are combined in *Lazarillo:* the soliloquy addressed to God, a confession written for a confessor, and a confession for the tribunal of the Inquisition.

At this point, however, Lazarillo has learned from experience what masters are like and how he will likely be treated. And the reader has learned with him. The reader also knows Lazarillo more intimately than do his masters. A liaison is established between Lazarillo and the reader, who side together against these unsympathetic and exploitative masters. The reader is not likely to share the blindman's or *clérigo* of Maqueda's opinion of Lazarillo, in that he comprehends Lazarillo's hunger, poverty, aloneness and alienation. Various *destinataires* then, besides God and Lazarillo himself, intervene between Lazarillo and the real reader. But it is clear that the reader is expected to react quite differently toward Lazarillo, and to reject the taskmasters' norms. The reader's mistrust of the world Lazarillo encounters is reinforced by Lazarillo's wariness. Lazarillo conceals from his cruel masters what he often reveals to his confidants, Vuestra Merced and the reader. Lazarillo carefully disseminates or withholds information depending on the person or persons addressed. Lazarillo and the reader criticize and reject a world distanced and satirized, but Lazarillo, unlike the reader, inhabits a fictional world that the reader need only view from afar or experience through a sympathetic identification with him. In order to survive, Lazarillo must come to terms with his environment.

Finally, Lazarillo reports the accounts of others about himself, as well as his reaction to them. Several of the episodes in *Lazarillo* assume a theatrical quality in that they are witnessed and reacted to by an audience, which includes Lazarillo himself. Both the blindman and the *clérigo* of Maqueda tell the story of Lazarillo's misdemeanors to gatherings of people. Lazarillo is in a way his own audience, listening with both delight and dismay to tales about himself, hence not so much a *destinataire* as an eavesdropper or *voyeur*. Lazarillo is held up to ridicule by his masters, but is able to join in their laughter and to see himself as others see him, to convert his pain into common pleasure. He is not only superior to his masters in insight —i.e., he sees more than they do— but also in compassion. There are many indications of Lazarillo's sympathetic emotional reactions to others. For example, he is able to feel sorry for the blindman when he is hurt, and to pity the squire's hunger.

Occasionally Lazarillo evokes a sympathetic response from the outside world. When the rent collector appears, the neighbors of the poor squire declare Lazarillo innocent and not responsible for the squire's debts. In the first three *tratados* the reader is also inclined to give Lazarillo the benefit of the doubt, for Lazarillo's innocence, sense of mischief and fun, and compassion make him attractive to the reader. In the brief *tratados* which follow, Lazarillo observes his world more than he interacts with it, and we do not know how his masters react to him. Yet in the final *tratado* adverse public opinion again provides the backdrop to Lazarillo's actions. «Mas malas lenguas, que nunca faltaron, no nos dejan vivir, diciendo no sé qué y si sé que veen a mi mujer irle a hacer la cama, y guisalle de comer. Y mejor les ayude Dios que ellos dicen la verdad» (p. 175). The unfavorable reaction and gossip provoked by his living arrangements with the priest's concubine is indeed the *raison d'être* of the narration's composition in the first place—to explain the *caso*. Lazarillo is now implicated in the adult world he once satirized, distanced by irony, and morally ambiguous. He is no longer the innocent child and victim of that world, to be pitied and laughed at.

Thus Lazarillo becomes an arch-dissembler on the world's stage, and we know how various audiences reacted to him. Indeed, he is an actor who adjusts his role to his audience and who learns from their reaction to him. He reports these reactions through Vuestra Merced to the real reader. On every level the *destinataire* is made a determining influence in the development of Lazarillo's narration, a narration which emanates from a single source and is told from a unique perspective, but which is progressively modified by the effect it renders, concealed and revealed according to its variegated roster of *destinataires*.

The Final «Tratado»: A New Vision of «Lazarillo»

The last *tratado* induces the reader to reflect upon the narration as a whole. The references to the *caso* direct him back to the beginning of a narration which he has heretofore experienced sequentially, identifying with or sympathizing with the first person narrator. The rather intimate account presented in the first three *tratados* offers a contrast to the superficial and/or summary treatment given to events in *tratados* IV, V, and VI. Here Lazarillo views himself from outside, explaining what happened without much detail about how he felt or what he thought. In the episode of the *buldero* his role is that of bemused observer, one not directly implicated or deeply affected by events. As usual, Lazarillo moves on from master to master, but by the sixth *tratado* he is (significantly) able to put aside a little money to buy himself a second-hand suit of gentleman's clothes. With this proper attire and some good luck, he procures the office of *pregonero* and acquires a wife. His situation now promises more security and permanence than ever before. In the beginning the *caso* provoked the curiosity of Vuestra Merced and provided the original impulse to Lazarillo's telling his tale. In the last *tratado* the reader realizes that the *caso* refers directly or indirectly to Lazarillo's marriage to the Archpriest's concubine, a scandalous arrangement to say the least. The whole of Lazarillo's narration, then, must be understod as a self-defense, for gossips accuse him of living as a cuckold and he is perhaps even in trouble with the law. His life story assumes the quality of an apology, as well as a confession and explanation. The contemporary reader, presumably superior in social status like Vuestra Merced and heretofore sympathetic to Lazarillo, must have felt doubly startled by Lazarillo's attitudes toward his marriage and profession. It would be difficult for him to regard Lazarillo as fortunate in being able to curry the favor of the Archpriest and in occupying the ignominious office of *pregonero*. Lazarillo, on the other hand, even associates his «success» with the rising good fortunes of the Spanish Empire. The reader is no longer able to relate to Lazarillo as an innocent victim satirizing a corrupt society they both abhor. Lazarillo has joined the world he once mocked. He now regards himself with the same irony once reserved for the world he suffered, or is by now so attuned to dissembling that he accepts his own pretence. The reader's responses to Lazarillo's tale, quite elaborately manipulated up to now, are finally subjected to a shock treatment. New knowledge of Lazarillo requires that the reader reflect and reevaluate the whole of Lazarillo's life. It is now apparent that the truth about him has many facets and at least as many refractions.

The ending of *Lazarillo* is surprising and ambiguous, rather than predictable, and places high demands on the reader's interpretive skills.[18] Indeed, *Lazarillo* might appeal to readers of various social backgrounds and from various historical periods in differing ways. For example, the sixteenth-century *cristiano viejo* and *converso,* holding views appropriate to their respective statuses, could hardly be expected to agree on the work's significance to them. I have suggested that one possible stance indicated for the reader in the work itself is that of Vuestra Merced, a curious listener of superior social status. But Lazarillo's tale must also have struck a chord with the frustrated or disenfranchized, particularly the *conversos,* who might have sided with Lazarillo against authority and Vuestra Merced. As Claudio Guillén points out, «a large literate audience of Spaniards around 1600 could not possibly coincide with the lower class. It was probably most akin not to the heroes of picaresque novels, but to their authors, particularly Mateo Alemán. Its core, in other words, would have been the discontented middle class. (Generally speaking, the rise of the novel in sixteenth-century Spain seems to have been rooted not in the triumph but in the frustration of the bourgeoisie.)»[19] Many sixteenth and seventeenth-century readers may have experienced economic insecurity or social ostracism or society's corruption, and therefore would have regarded Lazarillo as a kindred spirit. Moreover, readers would almost universally have had to relate to Lazarillo's life as one they would themselves have shunned. As Martín de Riquer points out,

> El *Lazarillo* es la biografía no deseable; nadie, sobre todo en España del siglo XVI, podía desear haber tenido un padre encarcelado por ladrón, una madre que se entrega al más vil morisco, haber pasado hambre, y sobre todo, tener una esposa compartida con un arcipreste. En la vida de Lazarillo se acumula todo aquello que nadie quisiera para sí, y su lectura interesa primordialmente a los que en modo alguno pueden ver en ella su retrato.[20]

In one way or another, both Guillén and Riquer posit a discontented readership that discovered in Lazarillo a fellow sufferer. However, another school of thought insists on the Renaissance reader's interpretation of the work as a «libro de burlas», and on a readership primarily consisting of «caballeros y cortesanos.»[21] There is also considerable disagreement on

[18] See Chapter I, page 29: Kermode makes a distinction between the structure of naive fiction which is based on traditional paradigms, and sophisticated fiction which departs from those paradigms. See also p. 25 in reference to Fish who distinguishes between rhetorical and dialectical presentation.
[19] GUILLÉN: *Literature as System*, p. 144.
[20] MARTÍN DE RIQUER: *La Celestina y Lazarillos* (Barcelona: Vergara Editorial, 1959), p. 108, quoted in RICO: «Introducción», p. XVI.
[21] See ALBERTO BLECUA: «Introduction to *La vida de Lazarillo*», pp. 35-38; CHE-

the extent of *Lazarillo*'s diffusion and popularity;[22] but it was placed on the Inquisition's list of prohibited books in 1559, a possible indication that some readers regarded the work as pernicious. On the other hand, the expurgated version published in Spain in 1573 suggests that the profound heterodoxy detected by many modern critics passed essentially unnoticed by the Inquisitors.[23]

Whether one regards *Lazarillo* as a funny or a nasty book depends on how one interprets the ending, and how one relates Lazarillo, the child, to Lázaro, the adult. Some of the discrepancies between individual interpretations, ancient and modern, may be due to assigning greater importance to one or another aspect of the work — in the same way that the blindmen in the old joke describe different parts of the elephant as the beast itself, because they perceive just one part and not the whole. Thus some critics emphasize the nasty and unctuous tone of Lazarillo, his corruption as an adult, his lack of credibility as narrator, or the ironic distance established between author and narrator; for Lazarillo is trying to persuade the reader of something that the author is not at all convinced of — that he has arrived at «buen puerto.»[24] Others, attributing primary importance to the folkloric sources of *Lazarillo*, stress the work's fundamental comicity.[25] Clearly, there are several levels and many truths to Lazarillo; he is both the child and the adult. His experience encompasses the most witty playfulness and dreadful misery. Yet a proper interpretation must, I believe, take into consideration the new context of the traditional comic material and the work in its totality.

VALIER: *Lectura y Lectores en la España del Siglo XVI y XVII*, pp .175-185. Chevalier suggests that the Renaissance reader accorded more importance to Lazarillo than to Lázaro, an emphasis reversed by Guillén and many modern interpreters who place Lázaro at the center of the work's gravity («La disposición temporal del *Lazarillo de Tormes*», HR, 25 (1957), 271.

[22] See A. RUMEAU: «Notes au *Lazarillo*», *Bulletin Hispanique*, LXVI (1964), 257-293; GUILLÉN: *Literature as System*, pp. 137-146; RICO: *La Novela Picaresca y el punto de vista*, pp. 95-100; CHEVALIER: *Lectura y Lectores...*, pp. 167-175.

[23] BLECUA: Introduction to *La vida de Lazarillo*, pp. 37-38.

[24] L. J. WOODWARD: «Author-Reader Relationship in the *Lazarillo de Tormes*», *Forum for Modern Language Studies*, I (1965), 43-53; ALAN DEYERMOND: «The Corrupted Vision: Further Thoughts on *Lazarillo de Tormes*», *Forum for Modern Language Studies*, I (1965), 246-249; ALFONSO REY: «La novela picaresca y el narrador fidedigno», *HR* (Winter 1979), pp. 55-75. FRANCISCO MÁRQUEZ VILLANUEVA: «La actitud espiritual del *Lazarillo de Tormes*», in *Espiritualidad y literatura en el siglo XVI* (Madrid: Alfaguara, 1968), pp. 69-113.

[25] MARCEL BATAILLON: *Novedad y Fecundidad del Lazarillo de Tormes* (Madrid: Ediciones Anaya, 1968), pp. 48 ff. HOWARD MANCING, in «The Deceptiveness of Lazarillo de Tormes», *PMLA*, 90 (May, 1975), 426-432, attributes optimistic or comic readings of *Lazarillo* to the author's skillful presentation of the beguiling boy and the reader's reluctance to recognize the base and morally corrupt adult discovered by a more careful reading. GÓMEZ-MORIANA in «La subversión del discurso ritual», pp. 79-83, considers the effect of including traditional comic material in an autobiographical confession subversive to the latter.

Mimesis and the Reader

The full range and diversity of Lazarillo's experience is skillfully brought home to the reader in other ways as well. Thus far I have discussed the roles the author indicates for the reader in the prologue and body of the narration, the way in which the inclusion of various *destinataires* guides reader response, and how the final *tratado* causes the reader to reevaluate the entire narration. Other aspects of the narrative process also induce the reader's empathetic response to Lazarillo's experience. Of particular importance are the manipulation of time, the use of significant particulars to exemplify general truths, and the emphasis on the material or sensual. Lazarillo shares his life's experience with the reader in such a way that it is concretized in the here and now world of the senses. Lazarillo's reactions to and interpretations of his experiences are never simplistic, but rich, various, and sometimes even contradictory. This is a life remembered, and the narration combines the immediacy of experience with the benefit of hindsight. Lazarillo's attitude toward his life is bemused, tolerant, and ironic, but not bitter. All reality is perceived through Lazarillo's memory and perceptions, but he is broad-minded in his views, a singular mind capturing many aspects and angles of things. As a character, Lazarillo appreciates the ambiguities of experience and reflects in his own attitudes rapid shifts in perspective. Thus he refers to the «dulce y amargo jarro,» sweet because it held the wine he siphoned off with a straw, bitter because it was later smashed in his face by the blindman, and values what he learned from the encounter — «mil cosas buenas me mostró el pecador del ciego.» Lazarillo records both the pleasure and the pain, the good and evil consequences of events, and thus the complexity of life. As a narrator who caters to many *destinataires,* he reproduces in his own version of reality a multiple perspective.

Lazarillo's retrospective account of his life, combining his immediate reactions to events as they occur and reflections from then and now, communicates to the reader a well-rounded and thus convincing view of reality. He draws from both his youthful and adult selves, or the intersection of two selves and two temporal planes. Another temporal dimension of the work is its pace or tempo. Time thickens perceptibly and events are recounted with agonizing slowness in the third *tratado,*[26] thus enabling the reader to fully experience both Lazarillo's physical discomfort and the development of his intricate relationship with the *escudero.*[27] Time moves most slowly at the novel's center, and the lives of the *escudero* and Lazarillo mirror one another in reverse. The *escudero* retains the illusion of honor but starves; Lazarillo at the narration's close has enough to eat but has lost his honor. In the third *tratado* Lazarillo is at his most sympathetic, able to feel pity and compassion for the *escudero* in spite of his own hardships. Lazarillo's physical discomfort, in particular his hunger, is given

---

[26] GUILLÉN: «La disposición temporal del *Lazarillo de Tormes*», pp. 264-279.
[27] DÁMASO ALONSO: «El realismo psicológico en el *Lazarillo*», in *De los Siglos oscuros al de Oro* (Madrid: Editorial Gredos, S. A., 1958).

an hour by hour detailed description against the backdrop of the *escudero*'s ridiculous pretenses. Throughout *Lazarillo,* the inclusion of the material and sordid aspects of his existence impart reality to the narration. The reader shares with Lazarillo the imaginary experience of those sufferings common to the human condition — hunger, discomfort, and pain. The use of sensual and physical description is in some respects quite singular in *Lazarillo.* For example, Lazarillo describes a sleepless night in the *escudero*'s house in the following way: «Porque las cañas y mis salidos huesos en toda la noche dejaron de rifar y encenderse, que con mis trabajos, males, y hambre, pienso que en mi cuerpo no había libra de carne» (p. 135). In this little passage two common narrative techniques of *Lazarillo* are exemplified: first, the use of exaggeration to express how he *felt* (on his body there was not a pound of flesh); second, the personification or humanization of mindless entities (his bones quarrel and become angry). A few sentences before he referred to his «hambriento colchón.» Thus human emotions and reactions are often attributed to things in Lazarillo's world, which is emotionalized through the use of epithets.[28] Lazarillo's value judgments and feelings become in a sense inseparable from the world itself, as people and objects become, as it were, electrically charged by his emotional reaction to them. He refers, for example, to «la negra honra del escudero,» «el pecador del ciego,» and so on. Lazarillo continually plays with and records the sensual aspects of existence — sights, sounds, scents, and feelings. Both the pleasant and the grotesque or repugnant are well represented, hence, «el sabroso olor de la longaniza» and later «su nariz y la negra, mal mascada longaniza a un tiempo salieron de mi boca» (p. 108). Often a sensually pleasant feeling of momentary contentment is swiftly undercut or undermined by some nastiness or other. What seems good at first is too soon not so, and misery swamps pleasure. The *altibajos de la fortuna* are graphically and dramatically projected. Lazarillo's emotions and value judgments thoroughly dominate our vision of his world. His point of view is of course partial to himself. Thus, and in some ways, Lazarillo's style contributes to making him an untrustworthy and manipulative narrator, yet an extremely skillful one; for he transmits his life's experience to the reader graphically, thus enhancing the reader's sense of participation. Some of the distance imposed on the reader through the work's network of fictional *destinataires* is erased by this concretization of sensual experience as well as by the sympathetic character of the protagonist as he is growing up.

Another aspect of the narration which draws the reader into its fictional world is its economy, its use of significant particulars. Lazarillo invites the reader to extract from the episodes recounted a generalized picture of a corrupt world. He does not tell all, but leaves gaps in the text for the reader to fill in. He indicates that he has carefully selected his material so that choice details exemplify the general quality of his life. Thus he prefaces an anecdote with statements such as «contaré un caso de mu-

[28] GULLÉN: Introduction to *Lazarillo de Tormes* (New York: Dell Publishing Co., 1966), p. 16.

chos» (p. 103), or «Mas por no ser prolijo dejo de contar muchas cosas así graciosas como de notar» (p. 106). Not only the episodes that occur but some of the characters that he encounters are implied to be typical. There is a strong tendency on the part of Lazarillo to interpret his world paradigmatically, to regard the singular as an example of a species, to think in terms of categories. Expressions such as «estos burladores» (p. 169), «alguno de su hábito» (p. 143), and «cuántos de aquestos» (p. 137), reinforce the idea that the comic figures represent types,[29] people of the sort we are all familiar with. As a narrator, Lazarillo convincingly depicts the material world of the senses, charged with his own emotions and generalized as though it were true.

Tradition and Innovation

An important aspect of aesthetic response depends on the reader's expectations as they are derived from past reading experience. Modern readers regard *Lazarillo* as an innovative work that initiated a new genre, yet its novelty must have been perceived quite differently by the Renaissance reading public. The work's debt to past literary works is many-faceted and includes both structural and ideological reminiscences. Contemporary fictional forms are both imitated and parodied, and some narrative material from the tradition of medieval satire is included and imbued with new meaning. In particular, the episodic structure of medieval romance and the humor of farce and folktale are combined and subtly transformed in Lazarillo' confessional letter to Vuestra Merced.

Both chivalric romance and saints' lives consist of an episodic series of adventures through which the romance hero proves his heroism and the saint his saintliness. Both are exemplary heroes, and their deeds and *modi vivendi* provide models of conduct which medieval readers were meant to admire and might have wished to emulate. An episodic structure also suits the characteristic picaresque activity and vision of the world. Like a saint or chivalric knight, the pícaro embarks on a quest and endures long-lasting trials and tribulations in order to justify his existence. However, the *pícaro* is rewarded for neither heroism nor sanctity; he does not even achieve his goal of social acceptance. Thus a tension is developed in the narration which is not resolved in the ending. The *desire* of the *pícaro* to find his place in society is well expressed by an episodic structure, but the impossibility of his success is suggested by the lack of resolution in most picaresque novels.

The picaresque novel preserves many features of romance,[30] but imparts to them a negative significance. The *pícaro*'s beginnings are a travesty of the chivalric hero's — a comment on their lack of reality. His mother is not a queen but a laundress (*Lazarillo*) or a courtesan (*Guzmán*) or a witch

---

[29] RICO: «Introducción», pp. LXIII-LXVI.

[30] Cf. FRANK W. CHANDLER: *Romances of Roguery* (New York: 1899); ULRICK WICKS: «The Romance of the Picaresque», *Genre*, XXI (1978), 29-44; FRYE: *Anatomy of Criticism*, pp. 186-206; EUGENE VINAVER: *The Rise of Romance* (New York and London: Oxford University Press, 1971).

(*Buscón*), and his father is not a king, but a thief, deviant, gambler, or pastry cook. *Lazarillo* initiates the convention of parodying the noble hero's geneology and birth. Like many a hero before him, Lazarillo is born near water; unlike any hero before him, he is born on a flour mill in the familiar, nearby, and not at all mysterious river that flows by Salamanca, the Tormes. Thus his name is Lazarillo de Tormes, a name similar in structure to that of the chivalric hero, Amadís de Gaula. Only Lazarillo is not from a far-away and exotic land. Rather he is rooted in the contemporary Spanish soil, humbly born and bred. His mother happens to be at the mill where his father works the day he is born, and thus the ordinary quotidian activities of his parents determine his birthplace. Reality, they say, is the negation of illusion.

Lazarillo is a subversive work both in regard to contemporary society and the norms of literature of the past, in that the ideals of the aristocratic social order expressed in romance are rejected. In keeping with that vision, the nature of the episodes which form the totality of the *pícaro*'s experience owe far more to the tradition of medieval farce and satire than to the heroic acts peculiar to chivalric romance and saint's lives. The anonymous author of *Lazarillo* preserved the structure of romance, parodied its beginning, made indefinite its ending, and radically changed the contents of the individual episodes. The *pícaro* does not embark on a series of adventures so much as suffer a series of confrontations from which he escapes having suffered humiliation. But in the process his tormentors are exposed in all their folly. Lazarillo as protagonist and narrator battled with a double-edged sword — in behalf of his own survival and against the myriad figures commonly satirized in medieval folklore and fiction. Most of these are traditional figures, and generally they masqueraded as devout and virtuous persons, for they held such offices, but were in secret mired in vice. Lazarillo exposes their hypocrisy, and this is both the result and the by-product of the knowledge he gains from his experience with the world. However, the author relativizes the satire by establishing an ironic distance vis-à-vis his fictional narrator.

Comedy and Satire in «Lazarillo»

The episodic structure of *Lazarillo* is not only common to various genres of medieval fiction but also to the tradition of Menippean satire, in particular Apuleius's *The Golden Ass*, which is often cited as a source or precursor of *Lazarillo*. Thus Lazarillo is quite likely positively inspired in both the form and content by classical satire while rejecting the values and vision of the world of medieval romance. Yet both various stock comic *characters* and comic *situations* from the medieval tradition are well represented in *Lazarillo*.

The folkloric sources of these are difficult to ascertain with exactitude,[31] and do not really matter for the purposes of this chapter. Suffice it

---

[31] On the folkloric sources of Lazarillo see: RICO: «Introducción», pp. XXIV-XLII; A. CASTRO: «Perspectiva de la Novela Picaresca», in *Hacia Cervantes* (Madrid: Taurus, 1967); MARÍA ROSA LIDA: «Función del cuento popular en *Lazarillo*

to say that analogues to the various anecdotes in *Lazarillo* have been found in medieval farce and *fabliaux*, jest books, and traditional stories. The characters satirized belong to the classic comic type of the imposter or *alazon*. Medieval dissemblers, it appears, were often clerics, their outward holiness masking an inner cynicism and greed. They are characters dominated by a ruling passion or in bondage to some fault, such as avarice or hypocrisy, and rarely deviate from their prescribed roles.[32] Five of the characters in *Lazarillo* — the blindman, the *clérigo* of Maqueda, the *buldero*, the *fraile* of La Merced, and the Arcipreste — have their roots in the medieval tradition of ecclesiastical satire.

The inclusion of this traditional comic material is surprising in the context of confessional discourse, and is one of several factors that render the truth of Lazarillo's tale suspect.[33] Only the blindman and the *escudero* are more complex than their medieval counterparts, and reflect attitudes, values, and issues pertinent to Renaissance society.[34] Since *Lazarillo* is a pseudo-auobiography and confession directed to an authority figure, the point of view differs from that of farce or even classical satire. Lazarillo suffers at the hands of all these dissemblers, and as their victim offers a unique perspective on their misconduct and mistreatment of him.

We are accordingly presented with both a generalized vision of an evil world — albeit a largely fictitious and traditional one — and the way in which a particular and unique individual reacts to it. Moreover, Lazarillo learns from his encounters with the various characters in the narration — from his mother, to «arrimarse a los buenos», from the blindman, how to get by in the world, from the *clérigo* of Maqueda, how hunger can sharpen the wits, from the *escudero*, how foolish is an exaggerated sense of honor, from the *buldero*, when to hold his tongue, and so on. Political treatises on the education of princes were a common genre in the Renaissance. But this is a mirror for rogues, not for princes. Because Lazarillo learns from experience, encounters some characters who are more complex than caricatures, and writes from the point of view of the victim, the work is often considered a precursor of the modern novel. One focus of any present or past reader's attention is Lazarillo's life, and how he changes according to what he learns from living. But I suspect that the Renaissance reader may have been especially impressed by the work's novel use of common structures of discourse — romance, confession, and treatises on education.

---

de Tormes», APCIH (1964), pp. 349-359; BATAILLON: *Novedad y Fecundidad del Lazarillo de Tormes*; FERNANDO LÁZARO CARRETER: «Construcción y sentido del L. de T.», Abaco, I (1969), 45-134.

[32] FRYE: *Anatomy of Criticism*, p. 168.

[33] GÓMEZ-MORIANA: «La subversión del discurso ritual», pp. 79-83.

[34] GUILLÉN: Introduction to *Lazarillo de Tormes*, pp. 19-20; RICO: «Introducción», pp. XXIII-XL.

The Significance of Comedy in «Lazarillo»

The use of parody and satire in *Lazarillo* is complex, and at times is characterized by medieval attitudes and at times by a more modern use of parody, this latter in that it seems to attack value systems and to be heuristic rather than cathartic in its intentions. As Bakhtin pointed out in his book on Rabelais, the Renaissance is a crossroads to the extent that two types of imagery coexist in several works, among them *Gargantua et Pantagrueul* and the *Quijote,* the imagery inherited from the folk culture of humor and contrastingly that which is based on a bourgeois conception of a completed atomized being with private and egotistical aims. In the first case, according to Bakhtin, the grotesque bodily images are regenerative. Some of the grotesque comic episodes in *Lazarillo* may be interpreted in this light, for example the episode of the *jarro de vino,* in which the blindman, after having smashed the jug on Lazarillo's head, cleansed his wound with wine and prophesied a fortunate future for him. However from other events, such as his confrontation with the stone bull or his observation of the *buldero,* Lazarillo learns the art of ironic detachment, cynicism, and a sense of his aloneness and individuality.

Bakhtin points out that the Renaissance conception of laughter was a serious one — i.e., laughter was regarded as one essential means to discovering forms of truth concerning the world as a whole. Laughter had a deep philosophical meaning and provided a point of view from which the world could be seen perhaps more profoundly, such as in Erasmus' *Praise of Folly.* Later philosophies of humor, such as those of Bergson and Freud, would emphasize its negative functions, particularly its links with suppressed aggression. After the seventeenth century, according to Bakhtin, the important and essential, i.e., history and persons embodying it (kings, generals, and heroes) could not be depicted comically. Laughter belonged to the lower genres and the lives of private individuals pertaining to inferior social levels.[35]

It seems to me that the insights of Bakhtin raise some important questions vis-à-vis *Lazarillo.* We regard *Lazarillo* with a bourgeois vision and seek to discover the origin of the novel, the inception of the individual's quest for social recognition, and the transformation of universal paradigms into the personal search for relative values. We tend to underplay its carnivalesque spirit, its use of grotesque bodily images, its comic use of medieval satire and farce. Yet if humor is philosophically significant and the comic is universally participated in — in other words if the *Lazarillo* is still written in the medieval spirit using the exemplary «I» that really signifies «we» or «I» as an example of mankind, we may still wonder why the story is told from his point of view, that of a victim of farce also rooted in the lower classes, and wonder whether contemporary readers regarded his predicament as common to the human condition or as a private difficulty due to his social position. Certainly it seems that both ways of

---

[35] BAKHTIN: *Rabelais and His World,* pp. 66 ff.

viewing Lazarillo are possible — that he is both a universal type, reacting to the hardships of life and vicissitudes of fortune as Everyman would, yet also representative of the oppressed.

In this regard it is perhaps useful to recall that Lazarillo enters into a dynamic relationship with the static, comic world of the traditional story. The situations in themselves are funny, but their cumulative effect in the life of an individual is not. Hence we are dealing with something of a hybrid. A reader's response would surely vary according to the aspect or portion of the novel in focus, its particular incidents or its totality. To a modern reader, the more serious ramifications of Lazarillo's position might resemble a dilemma confronting the protagonist of a modern novel and thus seem familiar. Yet the same material constituted a novelty and indeed a revelation to readers steeped in the medieval tradition. On the other hand, the comic episodes are perhaps novel to us but extremely familiar to Renaissance readers, perhaps even familiar enough to undermine the veracity of Lazarillo's confession. In either case, one's interpretation would depend on attitudes toward tradition and innovation. My guess is that to perceive the unfamiliar against the background of the familiar is the more striking experience, and that the inclusion of traditional comic episodes in a work ostensibly presented as a confession seemed quite revolutionary to some sixteenth-century readers. The comic spirit of the work is perhaps puzzling to modern readers, whereas Renaissance readers would have understood the carnivalesque participatory humor with ease. Viewed against the background of this tradition, Lazarillo's ability to laugh at himself is not so surprising.

I have mentioned before that because of Lazarillo's sympathetic character as a boy, the reader is inclined to identify with him and imagine that he might react like Lazarillo if faced with the same trying existence. In some respects, Lazarillo treats the reader as his equal. In effect, *Lazarillo* is an uncomfortable and dialectical work of art calculated to invite the reader to look at himself.[36] There are several instances where it is strongly implied that the reader is expected to regard the work as a mirror for his own folly, human weaknesses being universal. «Cuántos debe de haber en el mundo que huyen de otros porque no se veen a sí mesmos» (p. 94), Lazarillo remarks when his step-brother shows fear of his own father. When Lazarillo states in the prologue that he is no more saintly than his neighbors, one may suppose that his neighbors are not saintly. Of course one of his neighbors is his fictitious reader, Vuestra Merced. The reader is also reminded in the prologue that he shares with the author and Lazarillo the common desire for fame. Somewhat paradoxically, Renaissance egotism or individualism is universalized. Thus there are some indications that *Lazarillo* is to be read by a reader who is able to identify imaginatively with Lazarillo's predicament and share in his humanity.

Lazarillo is sometimes one of us, sometimes «worse than us.» I have tried to suggest that the attitude toward parody and humor perhaps differed in the Renaissance and is another factor which brought Lazarillo closer to

---

[36] Cf. M. J. Woods: «Pitfalls for the moralizer», p. 597.

the reader. Even for the modern reader, steeped in a tradition of more aggressive (including «sick») humor, the sort of distancing for farce to be effective is undermined in the picaresque. Since the narrator is also the victim, the jokes no longer seem so amusing. Lazarillo confronts a number of traditional comic types and in response he himself becomes another impostor. But he is an individual as well, one we know intimately enough so that he is sympathetic to us. Farce reenacted from the point of view of the victim loses some of its comic force. As Bergson pointed out, «Laughter is incompatible with emotion. Depict some fault, however trifling, in such a way as to arouse sympathy, fear, or pity; the mischief is done, it is impossible for us to laugh.» [37] In this regard, Lazarillo's distance from the reader is a key factor, and we have seen that this varies, mostly because of the intervention of various *destinataires* between Lazarillo and the real reader, providing the latter with a kaleidoscopic vision of reality or a shifting and varying perspective on the truth of Lazarillo's tale. Here again, the presence of Vuestra Merced is of utmost importance in reminding the reader that Lazarillo is telling his story in his own defense to a paternal figure representing authority. An ironic distance is interposed between Lazarillo and the real reader that enables him to recognize that the tale is not to be interpreted as objective truth. Rather the tale represents a partial truth, slanted to favor a particular individual. Sometimes the reader laughs *at* or *with* Lazarillo and sometimes draws back to view him with irony.

Wit, Subversive Language, and the Reader

Another factor that serves the purpose of distancing Lazarillo from the reader is the frequent use of witty language — wit or *ingenio* being another form of distancing in that it involves the emotions with the surface of language and glosses over the depths of experience. In keeping with the comic spirit of the work the author often uses those rhetorical figures and stylistic devices that most provoke laughter — periphrasis, antithesis, zeugmas, paranomasias, «delexicalizations», colloquial words, refrains, and pat phrases.[38]

The use of language and imagery is often polysemic, ironic, or irreverent in *Lazarillo*, and the reader's recognition of this depends on his knowledge of the colloquial language and the social and religious systems prevalent at the time. The sexual (and even homosexual) *double entendres* of the spare fourth and sixth *tratados* have recently been deconstructed by Harry Sieber and others.[39] Their assumption is that like interpretations were made by some early readers. Often words acquire unusual or un-

---

[37] Quoted in WYLIE SYPHER: *Comedy* (Baltimore: Johns Hopkins University Press, 1956), p. XVII.

[38] BLECUA: Introduction to *La vida de Lazarillo de Tormes*, pp. 40-41.

[39] See SIEBER: *Language and Society*, especially chapters III and VII on the fraile de la Merced; GEORGE SHIPLEY: «A Case of Functional Obscurity: the Master Tambourine-Painter of Lazarillo, Tratado VI», *MLN*, 97 (1982), 225-253; JAVIER HERRERO: «The Great Icons of *Lazarillo*: the Bull, the Wine, the Sausage, and the Turnip», *Ideologies and Literature*, 1, no. 5 (Jan.-Feb., 1978), 3-18, and «The Ending of *Lazarillo*: the Wine Against the Water», *MLN*, 93 (1978), 313-319.

expected connotations due to Lazarillo's inverted system of values so that their meaning is essentially ironic, as is conveyed in the use of the word «bueno» in phrases such as «salieron a buen puerto» or «arrimarse a los buenos.» [40] In the context of Lazarillo's world «los buenos» cannot possibly mean «the good people,» but rather refers to the well-to-do or rich. In general, Lazarillo is by necessity so highly motivated to achieve worldly success that his *modus vivendi* subverts commonly accepted moral or religious values.

The metaphor of inner light or illumination is a case in point. The concept is often introduced when Lazarillo learns something or has a new insight, and it is first used to describe Lazarillo's education by the blindman. As a spiritual guide to Lazarillo, the blindman occupies a position which is likened to God's: «después de Dios, éste me dio la vida y, siendo ciego, me alumbró y adestró en la carrera de vivir» (p. 97). Lazarillo is also inspired or enlightened by God, «el Espíritu Santo», and by his very hunger: «Me era luz la hambre, pues dicen que el ingenio con ella se avisa...» As Bruce Wardropper suggests in «El Trastorno de la moral en el Lazarillo»,[41] God's will or divine inspiration is often associated in Lazarillo's mind with his rising fortunes and the dubious methods by which he reaches his position of security. Toward the end of the first *tratado*, God blinds the understanding of the blindman («Dios le cegó el entendimiento al ciego»), so that Lazarillo can take vengeance upon him. In the second chapter, Lazarillo, «alumbrado por el Espíritu Santo,» is inspired to have a duplicate key made so that he can steal from the strongbox of the *clérigo* of Maqueda. The ironies are perhaps most striking in the final chapter: «Quiso Dios alumbrarme y ponerme en camino y manera provechosa» (p. 172), says Lazarillo before entering the service of the Arcipreste of S. Salvador. Thus Lazarillo interprets God in the light of his own understanding, and discovers signs of divine approval when most successful at advancing his material well-being.

Sometimes the repeated use of a semantically significant word may reflect the prevalence of new social values or economic structures. Edmond Cros suggests that the decline of feudalism, the rise of the city, and the resulting creation of a large class of urban poor inspired new attitudes toward poverty, which was now regarded as a social ill. The Christian act of almsgiving lost its value, as did the idea of the *sanctus pauper*. Indeed, the Christian idea of charity is inverted. The poor are not tolerated, are driven out of the city, «satanized».[42] The word «devil» and its derivations are used with great frequency in describing the blindman's and Lazarillo's behavior, colloquially to be sure. The blindman initiates Lazarillo into his service by knocking his head against the stone bull of Salamanca, «el

---

[40] ALBERT A. SICROFF: «Sobre el estilo de *Lazarillo de Tormes*», NRFH, II (1957), 157-170.

[41] *NRFH*, XV (1961), 441-447.

[42] EDMOND CROS: «Semántica y estructuras sociales en el *L. de T.*», *Revista Hispánica Moderna*, XXXIX, no. 3 (1976-1977), pp. 79-84; see also JAVIER HERRERO: «Renaissance Poverty and Lazarillo's Family: The Birth of the Picaresque Genre», pp. 876-886.

diablo del toro», and then offers him this advice: «Necio, aprende que el mozo del ciego un punto ha de saber más que el diablo» (p. 96). Lazarillo refers to the blindman's cruel tricks as «burlas endiabladas» and speaks of the devilish need, «falta endiablada», that the blindman inflicts on him. He blames the idea of stealing the blindman's sausage on the devil's inspiration: «Púsome el demonio el aparajo delante los ojos...» (p. 106). And the blindman, too, associates Lazarillo's little successes against him with the devil. «¿Qué diablo es esto, que después que conmigo estás no me dan sino medias blancas?» (p. 99), or on another occasion: «¿Pensáis que éste mi mozo es algún inocente? Oíd si el demonio ensayara otra tal hazaña. Santiguándose los que le oían...» (p. 102). Thus the knowledge and politics of survival of the poor are associated indirectly with the diabolical.

Honor is another value which is parodied and criticized in Lazarillo. The Ciceronian idea of honor («La honra cría las artes») is, in effect, juxtaposed to Lazarillo's caso de honra and the escudero's pretentious, foolish adherence to an outmoded code of honor. Paradoxically, fame or honor due to success in the arts is achieved by exposing the folly of the escudero and telling the tale of Lazarillo's dishonor. Religious and moral values are undercut or undermined in Lazarillo, twisted and treated with irreverence. The use of traditional situational comedy from the Middle Ages may be regarded as comic, cathartic, and non-subversive, but often the use of language in Lazarillo indirectly attacks or challenges values and concepts. This sharp-edged irony is both heuristic and destructive, and implies that the author held some heterodox views.

In a sense, Lazarillo is a liminal figure who demonstrates the falseness or hypocrisy of antiquated societal values; yet, as an individual, he lives in an imperfect world that he rejects, but cannot altogether desert, and therefore joins half-heartedly.

The duality of the comic and the ironic, and the differing ways in which Renaissance and contemporary readers respond to the comic, seem to me the factors most responsible for the ambiguity of Lazarillo, for they induce a spectrum of complex and profound reactions in the reader that cause him to ponder the work at length and question his own attitudes. The Renaissance reader's expectations, formed by reading confession or romance, would have been jolted by the inclusion of comic episodes, lower-class protagonist, irreverent use of language, and the many parodic elements. However, the subversiveness, in the modern sense of the word, is tempered for a number of reasons: first, because medieval comedy is cathartic rather than revolutionary, and criticism does not imply that change is to follow; secondly, because the use of a fictitious reader as an upper-class or authority figure allows the real reader to adapt an anti-subversive stance. Similarly, the use of numerous destinataires offers the reader various vantage points from which to regard Lazarillo, a shifting perspective from which to interpret his story, now close and sympathetic, now distant and judgmental. The knowledge that Lazarillo is speaking in his defense and trying to present as flattering a portrait of himself as possible relativizes his story. He is an unreliable narrator telling his personal «truth» and the extenuating circumstances of his life, in order that he may appear in a favorable light to those in power. The reader, for all the reasons mentioned, vacillates in his responses to Lazarillo and is both amused and outraged — drawn to the sympathetic boy in his humanity, repelled by the cynical adult — yet withal understanding his predicament. Both society and Lazarillo are the culprits. And Lazarillo is a culprit because society made him so. The strategies of the author make possible this multitude of mixed reactions on the part of the reader.

The two ways of interpreting Lazarillo alluded to in the prologue, the surface and deeper readings each of which may delight (see p. 39), may reflect this dichotomy between the comic and the ironic. The more superficial reaction to the text produces a carnivalesque, participatory, sympathetic reading of *Lazarillo* with the resulting catharsis of laughter. Those readers who read more reflectively will view both Lazarillo and his society with irony, detecting an unreliable narrator and an attack on contemporary society through satire and the subversive use of language. Thus the primary impact of the text and subsequent reflection upon it may yield contradictory or polysemic readings which the reader may attempt to reconcile, successfully or not, in his own mind. In effect, *Lazarillo* wavers between presenting a comic and an ironic perspective to the reader, and modulates the two in an extremely subtle way which no later picaresque novel exactly emulates or achieves.

CHAPTER III

GUZMAN DE ALFARACHE: A CONFLICTIVE APPROACH TO THE READER

«Lazarillo» and «Guzmán»

Whereas the narrator of *Lazarillo* addresses his autobiography to the real reader through the presence of a fictitious reader, Vuestra Merced, and the work shifts and changes in tone in response to a kaleidoscope of *destinataires,* nothing intercedes between Mateo Alemán's tortured and emotional harangue and the hypothetical reader. Guzmán de Alfarache's monologue is so affected by the reader's expected reaction to his autobiography that it bears resemblance to an imagined dialogue. The reader's part in this conversation is sometimes omitted from the narrative, yet reflected in the way the account progresses. Often, however, Mateo Alemán includes what he imagines to be the reader's response and his reaction to that. From the first moment the reader is placed in an accusatory or hostile position vis-à-vis the narrator, who correspondingly assumes a defensive posture.[1] This relationship is established early in the prologue where Mateo Alemán repeatedly discusses the theme of how dreadful it is to be treated with hostility. Later he addresses «el vulgo,» i.e., the ignorant masses, who have persecuted him in the past and from whom he anticipates more trouble in the future. He then directs himself to the discreet reader, a reader he hopes for but, judging from the tone of the main body of the narration, does not really expect. Guzmán is a narrator disappointed in and even tormented by his readers.

The images that Guzmán uses to describe what he fears are hyperbolic and even suggestive of a state of paranoia. They strikingly reinforce the impression that he views the world and its inhabitants as unfriendly and hostile. Whereas the author of *Lazarillo* seemed to suspect that some readers would not be pleased by his tale and that interpretations would vary, Mateo Alemán established a dialogue with the reader in which the anticipated reader response is sometimes aggressively critical. Guzmán is therefore always apologizing, making excuses, explaining, and trying to deflect the reader's scrutiny by digressing. Both the images and the twisted, tortuous form of the prose transmit the emotional preoccupations of the author/

---

[1] JOAN ARIAS: *Guzmán de Alfarache: The Unrepentant Narrator* (London: Tamesis, 1977), p. 13.

narrator. The metaphors selected are unusual and often lugubrious or violent in a sensual way and thus strike the reader with great emotional force — always from close range. Guzmán de Alfarache usually addresses the reader as «tú» or occasionally «vosotros,» rather than «usted» or the more formal «vuestra merced» as in *Lazarillo*. Furthermore, the art of distancing and the use of comedy and irony skillfully intermingled in *Lazarillo* are virtually absent in *Guzmán de Alfarache*.

The Prologues: The Discreet Reader and the «Vulgo»

The dedicatory preface sets the tone for the rest of the work. Mateo Alemán begins by discussing fear, in particular the fear that men experience when confronted with another's bad intentions. «De las cosas que suelen causar más temor a los hombres, no sé cuál sea mayor o pueda compararse con una mala intención.» [2] Mateo Alemán declares that those of low birth and unknown lineage («oscura sangre») have evil intentions, which are all the more dangerous since they often go undetected. These unkind individuals are variously described as poisonous snakes and hunters lying in wait that wound without our knowing whence came the hurt. From their deceitful and lethal clutches no one is safe. Mateo Alemán confesses that he has always feared those of ill intent, but on this occasion he is even more afraid than usual, having opened himself to censure by daring to dedicate his book to a powerful prince. He needs the protection of such a powerful prince, however, for he is like a weak and badly defended city resisting the furious forces of its enemies. The defensive posture and the expectation of hostility are already salient features of the narration, as is the expressed hope for protection from the powerful.

During the prologue, Mateo Alemán directly addresses his intended readership, rather than assuming the guise of his *pícaro*-protagonist, Guzmán de Alfarache. His dedication to Don Francisco de Rojas is followed by an address to the *vulgo*, a commonplace in prologues, conforming to the classical tradition of Horace and his *Odi vulgum profani*.[3] The taste and influence of the *vulgo* was a hotly debated issue in regard to the *comedia*,[4] but mention of them seems out of place in a lengthy prose narration. Presumably the *vulgo* constituted a sizeable proportion of a theater audience, but was for the most part illiterate. Mateo Alemán does not refer to the *lector vulgo*, but simply the *vulgo*. He then addresses the *discreto lector*, not the *lector discreto*. The placement of the adjective, indicative of its generic rather than partitive use, implies that for Alemán all readers are by nature discerning and intelligent, no doubt partly because they are able to read. In contrast, the *vulgo* represents the crass ignorance of the masses, a cruel

---

[2] MATEO ALEMÁN: *Guzmán de Alfarache*, edición, introducción y notas de Samuel Gili Gaya (Madrid: Espasa-Calpe, 1972), vol. I, p. 27. All subsequent references to *Guzmán de Alfarache* are to this five volume edition of the text and will be cited in the text itself as follows: (I, p. 27).

[3] JOSEPH L. LAURENTI: *Los prólogos en las novelas picarescas españolas* (Valencia: Artes Gráficos Soler, S. A., 1971), p. 41.

[4] See, for example, LOPE DE VEGA: *Arte nuevo de hacer comedias; La discreta enamorada* (Madrid: Espasa-Calpe, 1948), pp. 11-19.

and capricious public whose reprobation the writer of prose was only too grateful to escape.[5] The dichotomy *discreto/vulgo*, following Mateo Alemán, became a convention of Golden Age prologues to narrative prose works and was used to distinguish the acumen, prudence, and refinement of the reader from the ignorance and sensational tastes of the semiliterate. The «vulgo» may here increasingly refer to a new class of undesireable readers.

Mateo Alemán indirectly associates the *vulgo* with those of evil intention in his dedication to Don Francisco de Rojas.[6] However, his chief interest is in the state of mind and behavior of the *vulgo* and their effect upon him both as a writer and an individual, as we shall discover in the main body of the text. His address to the *vulgo* is emotional and heartfelt, though exaggerated, rather repetitive, and rhetorical. The destructiveness of the *vulgo* is stressed through a long series of rhetorical questions. There is seemingly no refuge from their malevolence. «¿Quién será el dichoso que podrá desasirse de tus rapantes uñas? Huí de la confusa corte, seguísteme en la aldea» (I, p. 31). To Mateo Alemán the *vulgo* represents the barbarous and ignorant public opinion that continually criticizes, censors, and destroys anything worthwhile. The *vulgo* is worldly, mired in vice, unable to comprehend truth or justice, and incapable of *desengaño*, that enlightened turning away from a world that is only illusion to thoughts of the profound and eternal. Thus it follows that the *vulgo* will not be able to properly appreciate or interpret literature. They may be diverted by the story, but they will not like or heed the moral instruction. Mateo Alemán addresses the *vulgo* in the following manner:

[5] That is the idea reiterated in Vélez de Guevara's prologue to the «mosqueteros de la Comedia de Madrid», in *El Diablo Cojuelo*.

«Gracias a Dios, mosqueteros míos o vuestros, jueces de los aplausos cómicos por la costumbre y mal abuso, que una vez tomaré la pluma sin el miedo de vuestros silbos, pues este discurso de *El Diablo Cojuelo* nace a luz concebido sin teatro original, fuera de vuestra jurisdicción, que aún del riesgo de la censura del leello está privilegiado por vuestra naturaleza, pues casi ninguno de vosotros sabe deletrear: que nacistes para número de los demás y para pescados de los estanques de los corrales, esperando, las bocas abiertas, el golpe del concepto por el oído y por la manotada del cómico y no por el ingenio.» ANGEL VALBUENA PRAT: *La novela picaresca española* (Madrid: Aguilar, 1968), p. 1639.

According to Vélez de Guevara, then, the written word is directed to an elitist reading public that differs radically from a theater audience, a public that appreciates written «ingenio» and need not be auditorily «struck» with the comic force of a concept or amused by slapstick. This reading public assimilates information by reading rather than listening, presumably knows how to spell, and will not whistle when displeased, at least within the author's hearing.

For other discussions of *el vulgo* and the reading public see: E. C. RILEY: *Cervantes' theory of the Novel* (Oxford: Clarendon Press, 1962), pp. 107-115; WHINNOM: «The Problem of the Best-Seller», p. 195; CRUICKSHANK: «Literature and the book trade», pp. 818-824; OTIS GREEN: «On the Attitude Toward the *Vulgo* in the Spanish *Siglo de Oro*», *Studies in the Renaissance*, IV (1957), 196-200.

[6] Mateo Alemán describes his fear of those of evil intention, then the evil intentions of the *vulgo*, then how he fears the *vulgo*, so that the *vulgo* and those of evil intention are at least indirectly associated. However, as I try to stress later in the chapter, the protagonist Guzmán relates to the outside world in ways that are strikingly similar and limited. Many others besides the *vulgo* have evil intentions.

Eres ratón campestre, comes la dura corteza del melón amarga y desabrida y, en llegando a lo dulce, te empalagas. Imitas a la mosca inoportuna, pesada y enfadosa que, no reparando en oloroso, huye de jardines y florestas por seguir los muladares y partes asquerosas.

No miras ni reparas en las altas moralidades de tan divinos ingenios y sólo te contentas de lo que dijo el perro y respondió la zorra. Eso se te paga y como lo leíste se te queda. (I, pp. 31-32)

The reference to a moral *exemplum* is clear. The vulgo enjoys the narrative or «outer shell of the melon,» but learns nothing of importance and ignores the «sweet fruit» of hidden meaning inside.

Mateo Alemán, then, amplifies the concept of *vulgo* to represent a type of reader whose praise he does not wish for or actively seek, because he will not interpret the work properly. Moreover, Mateo Alemán actually fears the *vulgo*, it would appear. The mere thought of the *vulgo* distresses him — as though he had just faced a bull (I, pp. 32-33). He seeks a more sympathetic reception from the *discreto lector,* and in his tolerance and intelligence shelter from the storm of the *vulgo*. In the final portion of his prologue to the *vulgo,* he makes clear that he has suffered at their hands and hopes that his contact with the *discreto lector* will have a healing effect on him: «Las mortales navajadas de tus colmillos y heridas de tus manos sanarán las del discreto, en cuyo abrigo seré dichosamente de tus adversas tempestades amparado» (I, p. 32). Thus, a pact is established between author-in-the-text and reader-in-the-text in which both are considered members of an intellectual and spiritual elite, an enlightened oligarchy in the dark sea of the ignorant majority. Mateo Alemán not only seeks the protection of a wealthy patron, Don Francisco de Rojas, but tries to establish the same sort of relationship with a tolerant, enlightened, powerful, and protective reader. He is victimized by the *vulgo* and appeals to the discreet reader for deliverance.

In this respect Mateo Alemán adopts a humble and obsequious attitude. He flatters the discreet reader whenever possible. «A su corrección me allano, su amparo pido, y en su defensa me encomiendo» (I, p. 33), he states in his prologue to him. The prologue to the *discreto lector* includes a number of commonplaces, and Mateo Alemán's ingratiating approach to the reader is not that unusual a feature of seventeenth-century prologues. He first apologizes to the reader for his unworthiness as a writer («rudo ingenio y cortos estudios» (I, p. 33)), but then, like Lazarillo, reminds the reader that something good can be found in any book («no haber libro tan malo donde no se halle algo bueno» (I, p. 33)). At the same time and somewhat contradictorily, he assumes that the reader is as eager to read his work as the writer is desirous of telling his tale. To this curious reader, who is also interested in self-improvement or deriving some advantage from the work's moral teachings, he addresses himself («tú, deseoso de aprovechar» (I, p. 33)). He points out that he carefully considered the *discreto lector* while writing his work («a quien verdaderamente consideré cuando esta obra escribía» (I, p. 33)). The aforementioned «escribía» implies that the prologue was composed after the first portion of the work, published in 1599, was completed. Unlike the anonymous author of *La-*

zarillo, Mateo Alemán does not explicitly hope to achieve fame and glory through his writings, although he certainly expresses worry about adverse public opinion and the effects of a bad reputation. His purpose in writing is rather educative or moral. He writes for the common good. To stress this particular point, he uses images of a ship arriving at port, which is faintly reminiscent of the final portion of the prologue to *Lazarillo* («... y cuánto más hicieron los que, siéndoles contraria, con fuerza y maña remando salieron a buen puerto»). It is as though he were rejecting an essential purpose strongly adhered to by the author of *Lazarillo,* that the work will demonstrate how a determined *pícaro* can, according to his own criteria, rise in the world. The aim of this work is quite different. Mateo Alemán uses the image of a boatman facing backward toward the shore of the picaresque narration, rowing forward toward the moral purpose or common good. He fears that the reader will misunderstand his intentions, and think he wants to disembark on the land of picaresque adventures.[7]

> Alguno querrá decir que, llevando vueltas las espaldas y la vista contraria, encamino mi barquilla donde tengo el deseo de tomar puerto. Pues doyte mi palabra que se engaña y a solo el buen común puse la proa... (I, p. 34)

In this passage Mateo Alemán typically answers to anticipated adverse criticism and denies its application. He is consistently concerned about the effect of his work and afraid that it may be misread. Some things, he later claims in the same passage, he has omitted, reported incompletely, or amended in order not to offend anyone.

Thus, in a number of ways Mateo Alemán reveals his apprehension about the reader's reaction to his work. He is fearful of mis-interpretation on the part of the *vulgo* and proceeds carefully lest he offend the finer sensibilities of the *discreto lector.* He assumes that one type of reader, symbolized by the *vulgo* and indirectly associated with evil, lower class, or badly intentioned people, will not appreciate the moralizing digressions of his work. The *discreto lector,* on the other hand, may disapprove of the work because it dwells on the adventures of a *pícaro* and therefore cannot be taken seriously. Mateo Alemán is concerned lest his work will please neither audience.

The moral purpose of *Guzmán de Alfarache* is often reiterated and the reader advised that he should read and interpret accordingly. «No te rías de la conseja y se te pase el consejo» (I, p. 34). A process whereby the reader can mentally convert the work's content to beneficial use is suggested: «Recoge, junta esa tierra, métela en el crisol de la consideración, dale fuego de espíritu, y te aseguro hallarás algún oro que te enriquezca» (I, p. 34). The reader is also instructed to read between the lines, for the author sometimes wrote obscurely, and to ponder the moral or philosophical

---

[7] CARROLL JOHNSON: *Inside Guzmán de Alfarache* (Berkeley, Los Angeles, and London: University of California Press, 1978), p. 31. Johnson interprets this passage as a reference to the danger that the *discreto lector* may think that Alemán is presenting the picaresque adventures for the purpose of entertainment, rather than instruction. The rower, facing backward, has his eye on the evil picaresque life, as he propels his boat forward toward the shore of moral instruction.

content of the work. The traditional medieval hermeneutics of deciphering hidden or secret meanings is required by this Baroque text. The *corteza* covers the *meollo,* the chaff conceals the wheat, and the narrative example embodies a moral purpose. The laudatory prologues and poems by illustrious readers which appear in the preface indicate that the work was interpreted as exemplary material, «ejemplo y dechado a los que se dispusieron a gozar semejante vida» (I, p. 39). The life of *Guzmán de Alfarache* provides a negative example not to be emulated:

> ... enseña por su contrario
> la forma de bien vivir (I, p. 43)

In the final section of the prologue composed by Mateo Alemán, «Declaración para el entendimiento deste libro,» the events that take place in each of the three volumes are briefly outlined. Mateo Alemán informs us that Guzmán is writing his autobiography on a galley ship, to which he has been sentenced to row as a slave for his crimes. Thus the work's ending is disclosed in the prologue and provides the *raison d'être* for its composition — to explain why and how Guzmán was condemned to the galley, so that the reader will avoid his example.

The Role of the Reader in the Narration Itself

In the first chapter Mateo Alemán's *pícaro*-protagonist, *Guzmán de Alfarache,* begins to narrate the story of his life, although there are periodic lapses wherein Mateo Alemán ignores his fictional identity and, as author, directly addresses the reader. In some long passages of philosophical digression, where rhetorical questions abound and moral generalizing occurs, it is actually quite difficult to distinguish author's and protagonist's voice. Other narrators, such as travelling companions, tell all the interpolated tales. Occasionally, the young Guzmanillo records his thoughts, as in the long passage on the joys of a picaresque life and the meditation on honor (II, pp. 43-54), but usually the mature Guzmán narrates from his perspective of bondage, affecting the guise of a repentant prisoner who has undergone a religious conversion. When another character narrates or the young Guzmanillo speaks, it is quite clearly indicated in the text.

A number of typical characteristics appear in the initial paragraphs of this pseudo-autobiography. In various ways Mateo Alemán assumes an emotional approach and, concurrently, employs elaborate rhetorical strategies to manipulate the reader's emotions.[8] Mateo Alemán attributes some stylistic defects, which he apologizes for, to his urgent desire to communicate his story to a likewise committed reader. On more than one occasion he answers to the reader's anticipated criticism of his work with explanations and excuses. Already the narrator's desired relationship with a discreet reader is undermined by his lack of confidence. The hypothetical reader is repeatedly told how he might react negatively or unsympathetically to

---

[8] ARIAS: *The Unrepentant Narrator,* p. 45.

Guzmán, thus preempting the spontaneous discovery of feelings vis-à-vis the narrator. The narration begins thus:

> El deseo que tenía —curioso letor— de contarte mi vida, me daba tanta priesa para engolfarte en ella sin prevenir algunas cosas que, como primer principio, es bien dejallas entendidas —porque siendo esenciales a este discurso también te serán de no pequeño gusto— que me olvidaba de cerrar un portillo por donde me entrara cualquier terminista, acusándome de mal latín, redarguyéndome de pecado, porque no procedí de la difinición a lo difinido y antes de contarla no dejé dicho quiénes y cuáles fueron mis padres y confuso nacimiento. (I, p. 47)

Later Alemán accedes to the wishes of his imaginary critic and does indeed begin by explaining the lives of his parents. Thus anticipated reader response is made to dictate the early development of the narration.[9]

In the second paragraph the dialogical structure and the defensive posture adopted are even more pronounced. Guzmán is now more apologetic about the content of the narration than its style, i.e., its convoluted beginning. The reason for the circumlocutions and hesitations seems to be mock embarrassment in response to the character and conduct of his father. In contrast to *Lazarillo's* first chapter «Cuenta Lázaro su vida y cuyo hijo fue,» here the title is «En que Guzmán de Alfarache cuenta quién fué su padre.» Guzmán's father is possibly one of the most fetchingly reprehensible parents created in a work of fiction, even though the shady character of the *pícaro's* parents became a common convention of most later picaresque novels. Guzmán feigns reluctance toward recounting the checkered career of his father, but enumerates many of the more lurid details with relish. He cites gossip about his father, then denies the truth of these rumors, equivocates, and demonstrates considerable ambivalence in his feelings. Many of the characteristics attributed to his father were those conventionally ascribed to *conversos* — for example, ostentatious display of religiosity, effeminate behavior, Italian background, and the practice of usury.[10] Before describing his father's life, Guzmán anticipates his reader's adverse reaction to his filial impiety.

> Y aunque a ninguno conviene tener la propiedad de la hiena, que se sustenta desenterrando cuerpos muertos, yo aseguro, según hay en el mundo censores, que no les falten coronistas. Y no es de maravillar que aun esta pequeña sombra querrás dellos inferir que les corto de tijera, y temerariamente me darás mil atributos; que será el menor dellos tonto o necio, porque, no guardando mis faltas, mejor descubriré las ajenas. Alabo tu razón por buena; pero quiérote advertir que, aunque me tendrás por malo, no lo quisiera parecer —que es peor serlo y honrarse dello— y que, contraviniendo a un tan santo precepto como el cuarto, del honor y reverencias que debo, quisiera cubrir mis flaquezas con las de mis mayores; pues nace de viles y bajos pensamientos tratar de honrarse con afrentas ajenas, como de ordinario se acostumbra: lo cual condeno por necedad de siete capas, como fiesta doble. (I, p. 48)

---

[9] For an excellent close analysis of this passage, see M. J. WOODS: «The teasing opening of Guzmán de Alfarache», *BHS*, 57 (1980), 213-218.
[10] JOHNSON: *Inside Guzmán*, pp. 165-167.

Thus the narration begins heavily laced with the reader's hypothetical criticism. The reader-in-the-text accuses, and Guzmán overwhelms and diverts him with elaborate circumlocutions. Moreover, the reader's responses are prescribed, before he is provided with sufficient information to assess events independently.

Further subtleties in Guzmán's relationship with the reader come to light from a study of the following questions. The first concerns the degree to which the ideal reader described in Mateo Alemán's prologue resembles the reader portrayed in the body of the narration. The second question, related to the first, pertains to when, how, under what circumstances, and why Guzmán de Alfarache directly addresses the hypothetical reader. The third involves the nature of the real reader's relationship to the hypothetical reader. What emerges is a picture of a narrator who doubts that the reader can properly fulfill his role. Alemán obsequiously addressed an understanding, sympathetic, and discreet reader in the prologue. His expectations, however, are not consistently sustained or realized in the course of the narration, during which Guzmán's attitude toward the hypothetical reader vacillates tremendously. Often Guzmán regards the reader as a mortal enemy, and less frequently as a friendly travelling companion on the journey of life.[11] (For examples of the latter, see Vol. III, pp. 69 and 220.)

When and How Guzmán Addresses the Hypothetical Reader(s)

The reader's imagined reaction to Guzmán's assertions often figures in the narration as means to argue some point with Guzmán. The reader's principal role in the text is to disagree. At times Guzmán carries on a long hypothetical conversation with the reader in which he answers to the reader's objections and the reader introduces new ones. There are numerous examples of these debates scattered throughout the text. (See, for example, I, p. 59; V, p. 42; IV, pp. 87-88; and III, pp. 69-74.) One such sustained dialogue occurs after Guzmán has lost his court case against his former servant, Alejandro, who had absconded with his money and clothes (III, pp. 264-267). Guzmán's only consolation for his humiliating defeat and subsequent imprisonment is to think of Judgment Day, when the poor will be recompensed. The worldly reader reacts with teasing skepticism; he invites Guzmán to entrust him with some of his money, to be paid back on Judgment Day of course. Guzmán retaliates by suggesting that Judgment Day may arrive before the reader is prepared:

> Querrásme responder: ¡Pues para ese día fíame otro tanto! ¿Tan largo se te hace o piensas que no ha de llegar? No sé. Y sí sé que se te hará presto tan breve que digas: Aun agora pensé que sacaba los pies de la cama: y será ya cerrada la noche. (III, pp. 264-265)

The reader introduces another objection — that the stolen goods were found, not rightfully earned, by Guzmán due to the special circumstances

---

[11] ANGEL SAN MIGUEL: *Sentido y estructura del Guzmán de Alfarache* (Madrid: Gredos, 1971), p. 233.

in which he was placed when he served the ambassador. Guzmán replies that one's money cannot be legally snatched away even if gained in an illicit or unsavory manner. He cites the earnings of the prostitute and the bandit by way of example, whereupon he resumes his sermonizing. He reminds the reader that Heaven is preferable to Hell, and that under certain circumstances salvation is impossible in any case:

> ... Mas es menester mucho para salvarse y será imposible salvarte tú con la hacienda que robaste, que pudiste restituir y no lo hiciste por darlo a tus herederos, desheredando a sus proprios dueños... No son burlas. No las hagas, que presto las hallarás veras. Testigo te hago de que te lo digo... (III, p. 266)

Here the hypothetical reader is warned that he would be condemned were he to rob someone else's estate; that is, he is cast in the role of potential sinner.

These speculations are abruptly interrupted by Guzmán's acknowledgment that the reader reads for pleasure and not to be indoctrinated. He apologizes for his tendency to sermonize, which is as irrepressible as the drunkard's desire to drink. If the reader has not been pleased by the aforesaid, Guzmán invites him to write something himself for Guzmán to consider:

> ¡Oh, válgame Dios! ¡Cuándo podré acabar comigo no enfadarte, pues aquí no buscas predicables ni dotrina; sino un entretenimiento de gusto, con que llamar el sueño y pasar el tiempo! No sé con que disculpar tan terrible tentación, sino con decirte que soy como los borrachos, que cuanto dinero ganan todo es para la taberna. No me viene ripio a la mano, que no procure aprovecharlo; empero, si te ha parecido bien lo dicho, bien está dicho, si mal, no lo vuelvas a leer ni pases adelante. Porque son todos montes y por rozar. O escribe tú otro tanto, que yo te sufriré lo que dijeres. (III, pp. 266-267)

The preceding conversation typifies many of the exchanges with the reader in other passages. He argues with the reader and defends himself from the reader's criticisms. He preaches to the reader, either admonishing him or else inviting him to heed his advice. Though the emotional pitch of the passage cited is relatively tranquil, this benign approach to the reader is the exception rather than the rule. Often the relationship established between narrator and reader is more abrasive, serious, and emotionally intense, reflecting Guzmán's suspicious and untrusting nature. The tone of his sermonizing varies from light-hearted to menacing; mild recommendations alternate with stern threats.

At the same time, Guzmán reveals an embarrassed preoccupation with the style and content of the work — chiefly its long-winded moralizing digressions — by apologizing, as in the passage above, by frequently asking the reader's permission to continue, and by registering disappointment when the reader denies that permission. Sometimes he acknowledges their doubts, but nonetheless continues to preach: «¿Diré aquí algo? Ya oigo deciros que no, que me deje de reformaciones tan sin qué ni para qué. No puedo más; pero sí puedo» (V, p. 42). Otherwise, as in the passage where

71

he discusses *mohatreros,* the writers of fraudulent sales contracts, he reluctantly modifies his account in deference to the reader's preferences:

> ¿Queréisme dar licencia que les dé una gentil barajadura? Ya sé que no queréis y, porque no queréis, en mi vida he hecho cosa de más mala gana que hacer con ellos la vista gorda, dejándolos pasar sin que dejen prenda.
> Mas porque no digan que todo se me va en reformaciones, les doy lado...
> (IV, p. 236)

In the examples just considered one may suppose that Mateo Alemán is indirectly poking fun at his garrulous protagonist.

More often than not, the reader that Guzmán addresses in the body of the text reacts more like the *vulgo* described in the prologue than the *discreto lector,* preferring entertainment to instruction, or fable to the moral teachings. Naturally this sort of reader would complain about the lengthy digressions containing moral and religious doctrine. Furthermore Guzmán seems well aware that his work merits criticism in a number of respects. He desires, but does not expect, the reader's patience and indulgence. With the exception of the prologue to the *discreto lector,* the reader that Mateo Alemán imagines in the course of the narration is almost never praised.

Groups or Categories of Readers Addressed

Periodically, Guzmán addresses specific social groups, rather then the reader *per se.* The earliest example of this occurs in the description of the life of his father, who is a merchant, in which Guzmán postulates an adverse reaction to him on the part of the merchants. They will think that he is not suitably qualified to discuss their profession:

> Alguno del arte mercante me dirá: «Mirad por qué claustro de pontífice y cardenales va votado. ¿Quién mete al idiota, galeote, pícaro, en establecer leyes ni calificar los tratos que no entiende?» (I, p. 59)

Guzmán is continually preoccupied that he will be mistrusted as an unworthy and unreliable narrator because he is a *pícaro* and a galley slave. Here and in other places in the text Mateo Alemán is compensating for an inconsistency in the character of the protagonist. His narrator is a beggar and servant who offers learned opinions on moral and theological issues. Mateo Alemán describes Guzmán in «Declaración para el entendimiento de este libro» as «un hombre de claro entendimiento, ayudado de letras y castigado del tiempo, aprovechándose del ocioso de la galera» (I, p. 36). In order to make the learned style of his rogue seem more verisimilar, he emphasizes Guzmán's university education and knowledge of Latin, Greek, and Rhetoric.[12] The contradictory character of the literary *pícaro* — a wise and highly educated rogue and thief — is a formal requirement of the picaresque novel, usually a pseudo-autobiography narrated exclusively by the rogue. Guzmán's qualifications as a man of letters are stressed in the prologue, but his moralizing purpose is really not explained

[12] JOHNSON: *Inside Guzmán,* pp. 11-12.

as a natural extension of his character until the end of the novel. Then we learn that he has undergone a religious conversion, and is thus a repentant *pícaro*, albeit his sincerity is open to question.

When directly addressing a specific social group, Guzmán often sermonizes, assuming an accusatory or superior tone. Guzmán rarely approaches the general reader in so combative a fashion. His most adamant accusations are reserved for those guilty of a particular vice.[13] As someone poor and needy, Guzmán admonishes those who live lavishly: «Oh epicúreo, desbaratado, pródigo, que locamente dices comer tantos millares de ducados de renta» (II, p. 10). In another passage the rich are exhorted to give alms and not to worry whether the poor are genuinely needy. The rich should always be generous, for charity is Christian and avarice is a vice (II, pp. 230-231). Guzmán often reverses roles with the critical reader in the sense that he criticizes and moralizes in return, rather than habitually apologizing for his own inadequacies.

Such is his attitude toward women, based on his own unlucky experience. Guzmán digresses at length on the vices, foolish expectations, and bad habits of women when they marry (IV, pp. 231-261). His point of departure for these speculations is his own marriage, which began in wealth and happiness and ended in poverty and disillusion. As is often the case he generalizes, making his particular experience the basis for his view of reality. He discusses at length women who cease loving their husbands after economic disaster strikes. Guzmán eventually becomes so emotionally involved with his recollections that he imagines a lively conversation between an interrogator — at first the reader perhaps, later himself — and a woman relieved by the death of her poverty-stricken husband:

> Comiénzanse a marchitar las flores, acábaseles la fuga, el gusto y la paciencia. Hacen luego un gesto, como quien prueba vinagre. Y si les preguntásedes entonces qué tienen, qué han o cómo les va de marido, responderán tapándose las narices: ¡Cuatrodiano es! ¡ya hiede!, no alcen la piedra, no hablemos dél, dejémoslo estar que da mal olor, trátese de otra cosa. (IV, p. 242)

These statements call for a direct answer from Guzmán, and he leaves off generalizing about what «they» will say. He sarcastically addresses but one wife, as «tú», associating her husband with that personification of poverty, Lázaro:

> Pues cómo, ¡cuerpo de mi pecado! ¡señora hermosa! No se queja Lázaro en el sepulcro de tus miserias, de donde no puede salir, dentro de las oscuras y fuertes cárceles, en el sepulcro de tus importunaciones, envestido en la mortaja de tu gusto, que siempre te lo procura dar a trueco, riesgo y costa del suyo, ligadas las manos y rendido a tu sujeción, tanto, cuanto tú lo habías de estar a la suya. (IV, p. 242)

---

[13] ANGEL SAN MIGUEL, p. 234, in his analysis of the way Guzmán approaches the reader, cites several examples where Guzmán accuses the reader. However, he does not point out that all of these accusations are in fact directed to specific groups.

The two passages just cited are good examples of the difference between Guzmán's narrating and sermonizing styles. The direct, humorous, colloquial speech of the women offers a contrast to the rhetorical sermonizing of Guzmán. He continues to discuss women and their reasons for marrying in the first place, now describing «them», now addressing one among them as «tú», at times reporting his own experiences, at times enlisting the reader in unearthing these truisms so that married people may be warned of their folly.

> ... saquemos a plaza las intenciones de algunos matrimonios, tanto para que se desengañen de su error las que por tales fines los intentan, como para que sepan que se saben, y es bien que les digamos lo mal que hacen... (IV, p. 245)

When addressing the misguided lady as «tú», Guzmán uses the «vosotros» form to address the reader (or perhaps all people in general as opposed to just women). He later switches to third person again to generalize about the nature of the lady's transgressions:

> Hermana, que son caminos ésos del infierno. Que te llevará Dios el marido, por tus disoluciones y desvergüenzas, para que con ese azote seas castigada, saliendo en pública plaza tus maldades. En la balanza que trujiste la honra dél andará la tuya presto. Mas mirad a quién se lo digo ni para qué me quiebro la cabeza. No temió a su marido, perdió a Dios la vergüenza y quiérosela poner con estos disparates, que no son otra cosa para ella. (IV, p. 256)

Other Destinataires in «Guzmán de Alfarache»

The frequent shifting from one person to another and the consequent change in perspective is a fundamental stylistic feature of *Guzmán de Alfarache*. The narrator, Guzmán, repeatedly switches the circuits of communication, as it were. He directs himself to the reader or to a third party, singular or plural, usually treating the reader as an antagonist, but occasionally as an ally («Let us...») The reader or a third party, singular or plural, may answer to Guzmán. Guzmán sometimes soliloquizes. These changes occur rapidly and often. The reader is at times even presented with alternative sources for the opinions proffered: «Estuvo preso por lo que tú dices o a ti te dijeron...» (I, p. 60). Guzmán projects the image of narrator who is anxious, obsequious, and extremely eager not to offend whomever he addresses in these imagined conversations. In several respects, then, the text of *Guzmán de Alfarache* is a monologue in which imagined dialogue in one form or another predominates,[14] a halting exchange between himself and a multitude of *destinataires*.

Guzmán does not always sustain a dialogue with the reader or a particular social group, but sometimes addresses an unspecified interlocutor (see, for example, II, p. 32). At times it is difficult to ascertain whether the «tú» in question be the reader or an impersonal «you» in the sense of «one», i.e., anyone who finds himself in that particular situation. It seems to me that this ambiguous «tú» is addressed in Guzmán's descrip-

---

[14] JOHNSON: *Inside Guzmán*, pp. 47-53.

tion of prison life, which he experiences first hand after losing the court case against Alejandro. Whether the «tú» refers to the reader or to Guzmán and others like him in prison, the effect on the reader is much the same. He is privy to the victim's perspective on incarceration. Thus, in an even more dynamic way than in *Lazarillo,* the reader vicariously suffers the misfortunes of the *pícaro* and must imagine himself in the *pícaro's* place. Guzmán describes in detail what happens to a man when he enters prison, beginning with the encounter with the *corchetes.* The eagle is kinder to the rabbit he carries away in his claws, states Guzmán, using one of his frequent allusions to the crueler aspects of the animal world to describe human relationships.[15] He continues thus:

> Daránte codazos y rempujones, diránte desvergüenzas, cual si tú fueras ellos, y no más de porque con aquello dan gusto a su amo y es costumbre suya, sin considerar que ni él ni ellos tienen más poder que para llevarte a buen cobro preso, sin hacerte injuria. Desta manera te harán ir a el *retro vade,* a la cárcel.
>
> ¿Quieres que te diga qué casa es, qué trato hay en ella, qué se padece y cómo se vive? Adelante lo hallarás en su proprio lugar; baste para en éste, que cuando allá llegues —mejor lo haga Dios— después de haberte por el camino maltratado y quizá robado lo que tenías en la bolsa o faltriquera, te pondrán en las manos de un portero y de tal casa, que, como si esclavo suyo fueras, te acomodará de la manera que quisiere o mejor se lo pagares.
>
> Mal o peor has de callar la boca, que no estás en tu casa, sino en la suya y debajo del poder, etcétera. (III, pp. 274-275)

Guzmán must be addressing the reader in the beginning of the second paragraph cited. In the rest of the passage one must suppose either that the *destinataire* is consistently the reader or that the identity of «tú» is ambiguous — Guzmán himself, an impersonal «you» or «one», or anyone in that situation, possibly including the reader.

Often Guzmán does hold an inner conversation with himself — tortuous monologues in which, as usual, he airs his doubts, agonizes over a decision, admonishes himself for his long-winded prose style, and moralizes. There are numerous examples of this soliloquizing in the section wherein young Guzmanillo speaks of honor and the pleasures of a picaresque life (II, p. 31-54). Even when Guzmán addresses no one in particular, his prose is heavily laden with rhetorical questions and emotional exclamations that invite some sort of answer, a salient example of the phenomenon observed by Bakhtin (see pages 25-26). Response is always suggested, or evoked, or anticipated, or taken into consideration, or imagined. Thus the process of the work is dialogical, an unending argument in which a proper synthesis of various contradictory elements is never achieved. The text is rather like a conversation between two antagonists who cannot resolve their quarrel.

---

[15] See JOSEPH SILVERMAN: «Plinio, Pedro Mejía y Mateo Alemán: La enemistad entre las especies hecha símbolo visual», *Et Cetera,* n. 14 (1969), 23-31.

Example and Sermon in «Guzmán de Alfarache»: «Conseja y Consejo»

Guzmán reflects and generalizes about the narrative material; and in a sense a division is established between the acts of his life and their interpretation. The narrative voice and the critical voice — the role of critic being played by various specific social groups, interlocutors, the reader, and Guzmán himself — represent two poles of an unresolved debate. Doctrine alternates with the tale of the material survival of the *pícaro* in an unjust world. Example is juxtaposed to sermon, and both are found wanting. Guzmán, as the narrator of a fiction, responds to the presence of a critical other who assumes myriad identities, only one of which is the reader. He projects a similar relationship on whomever he encounters. Johnson, in his *Inside Guzmán de Alfarache,* postulates that Guzmán is really talking to himself at all times,[16] an idea that correlates with the Lacanian concept of the other as in some way a projection of one's self.[17] What one rails against or ascribes to others, or defines one's self in relation to, must be considered as an integral part of one's self and accounted for. Thus the moralist cannot be understood except in the context of that which he condemns.

Furthermore, the roles in which Guzmán casts his interlocutors are largely similar or limited to certain specific configurations or recurring patterns. Guzmán apologizes to a critical reader, the *discreto lector,* who does not find the *pícaro* a reliable narrator. He defends himself from the reader who wishes only to be entertained, *el vulgo,* and apologizes for so much moralizing. But he also preaches to, admonishes, and criticizes the reader.

Two well-differentiated styles are often reflected by the narrating and moralizing selves of Guzmán, the former being clear, simple, colloquial, and metaphorically rich. The latter is didactic, rhetorical, baroque, and somewhat pompous, and, as such, reminiscent of emblematic literature and corresponding to Guzmán's critical and accusatory selves.[18] Guzmán as a fictional character is not altogether sympathetic, being rather whining and paranoid. However, his tales are spicy and appealing and his satire has the proper bite. The narrative material is realistic enough that the reader is emotionally captivated and is inclined to ask himself: If I were Guzmán would I not have responded in the same way under the same circumstances? The reader's enjoyment is participatory, but the *conseja* is followed by the *consejo,* heavy rhetorical sermonizing that is quite at variance with the tone of the narrative material. The meaning of *Guzmán de Alfarache* must derive from the alternation or confrontation of the two worlds depicted and the effect of each on the reader.

---

16 JOHNSON: *Inside Guzmán,* p. 52.

17 JACQUES LACAN: *The Language of the Self,* trans., Anthony Wilden (1956; rpt. New York: Dell Publishing Co., 1968).

18 CELINA S. DE CORTÁZAR: «Notas para el estudio de la estructura del *Guzmán de Alfarache*», *Filología,* VIII (1962), pp. 89-90.

The Second Prologue

Mateo Alemán's fear of reader reaction may be understandable in the first volume, published in 1599, since the work contained controversial material. His apprehensions proved to be unfounded in one sense, however, for *Guzmán de Alfarache* was one of the first authentic best sellers in the history of literature.[19] In the prologue to the *Segunda Parte,* published in 1604, it is claimed that 50,000 copies and 26 editions of the *Primera Parte* had already been printed in Spain and that the work had also been widely translated abroad (III, pp. 58-59). In spite of this success, there is little change in Guzmán's defensive approach to the reader in the *Segunda Parte.* He apologetically addresses the reader in the first chapter, hoping that his moralizing will not be interpreted as lack of respect. He anticipates that the reader will accuse him of proceeding with stupidity. He states that he is evil, and poisons all that he touches:

> Perdona mi proceder atrevido, no juzgues a descomedimiento tratarte desta manera, falto de aquel respeto debido a quien eres... Hablando voy a ciegas y dirásme muy bien que estoy muy cerca de hablar a tontas, pues arrojo la piedra sin saber a dónde podrá dar... Mas como soy malo, nada juzgo por bueno: tal es mi desventura y de semejantes.
> Convierto las violetas en ponzoña, pongo en la nieve manchas... (III, pp. 69-70)

Guzmán reiterates several times that the reader may suppose that because he himself is bad, his advice is not worth heeding. The self-deprecating tone of this lengthy dialogue with the reader continues for several pages. In other words, and just as in the *Primera Parte,* Guzmán methodically anticipates and answers to every conceivable objection the reader might have to his book. However, he does not distinguish in the prologue between the *discreto lector* and the *vulgo,* and in the first chapter he mentions several times the reader's human frailty and implies his propensity for sin. The reader is not addressed as though he were someone superior, rich, and powerful, but rather as a fellow human who stands to be aided by Guzmán's example.

Mateo Alemán's success as a writer, then, has done nothing to alleviate Guzmán's fears as a narrator, which might prevent one from identifying too closely the author's and the narrator's voices. Indeed Guzmán is recurrently on edge throughout the work. As a narrator, he fears the reader's scorn; as a protagonist, he is often frightened of attack, pursuit, or capture by the other characters in the fiction.[20] Guzmán relates to the reader as to the outside world, with irrational and unfounded fear. In contrast to Lazarillo, who adjusted his account and its disclosures to the particular *destinataire,* Guzmán does not dissemble or play to his audience. He consistently imposes the same relationships on everyone and everything he encounters.

[19] CLAUDIO GUILLÉN: *Literature as System,* p. 143; WHINNOM: «The problem of the Best-Seller», p. 193.
[20] JOHNSON: *Inside Guzmán,* pp. 93-95.

The Watchtower («Atalaya de la Vida Humana») and the Reader

Two quite legitimate complaints are voiced in Mateo Alemán's prologue to the reader in the *Segunda Parte*. The publication of an apocryphal *Guzmán* by a Valencian writer who used the pseudonym Mateo Luján de Sayavedra usurped much of Mateo Alemán's original material. Mateo Alemán rewrote the *Segunda Parte* to include another *pícaro*, Sayavedra, a vengeful parody of Luján's protagonist, and expressed resentment in the prologue against this blatant theft and plagiarism. His other complaint concerns the preference of the reader for fables rather than the moral lesson. In the prologue Mateo Alemán re-emphasizes, using new images, the fundamental relationship that exists between narrative material and doctrine and the purpose of the work:

> ... lo que con su vida en esta historia se pretende... es descubrir como atalaya toda suerte de vicios y hacer atriaca de venenos varios, un hombre perfecto, castigado de trabajos y miserias, después de haber bajado a la más ínfima de todas, puesto en galera por curullero della. (III, pp. 52-53)

Atalaya is a watchtower or sentinel stationed in such a watchtower, whose special vantage point enables him to warn others of dangers which they themselves may not be able to see. Guzmán's experience of vice should eventually work on him like an antidote to poison concocted from the poisons themselves. Life to Guzmán is a long and arduous journey through a sea of troubles. Guzmán has made such a journey so that the reader may profit from his experience.[21] Guzmán, in effect, suffers in the reader's place:

> Yo aquí recibo los palos y tú los consejos en ellos. Mía es la hambre y para ti la industria, como no la padezcas. Yo sufro las afrentas de que nacen tus honras. (III, p. 71)

He hopes that the reader, who is just as mortal as he («que hombre mortal eres como yo,» (III, p. 73)) will learn from his mistakes and not repeat them. The hoped for effect of the book on the reader bears some resemblance to the Aristotelian idea of catharsis. Reading of violence and evil will not incite the reader to imitate the actions depicted. Rather, according to some interpretations of Aristotle, the reader's vicarious emotional involvement with a fiction may purge him of a possible tendency to violence in real life. Alemán's idea seems repressive, as well as cathartic. The reader stands to be warned by Guzmán's hardships; *fear* of undergoing his suffering should prevent the reader from imitating his life.

---

[21] STANLEY FISH, in *Surprised by Sin* (London, Melbourne, and Toronto: Macmillan, New York: St. Martin's Press, 1967), pp. 1-56, attributes a similar narrative structure to MILTON's *Paradise Lost*. A dichotomy exists between the descriptions of Satan, who is depicted as an attractive and appealing superman, and the moralizing warnings which follow. The reader is sensually attracted to Satan, intrigued by his activities, and fooled by his rhetoric; then he is admonished by the author/narrator to beware of his seductive evil.

Guzmán mentions the image of the watchtower again later in the same book. He accuses his readers of misinterpreting the *Primera Parte* by concentrating more on the *conseja* than the *consejo*. Also, both men and books acquire bad reputations, and are misunderstood when falsely labeled. «Esto proprio le sucedió a este mi pobre libro, que habiéndose intitulado: *Atalaya de la vida humana,* dieron en llamarle *Pícaro* y no se conoce ya por otro nombre» (III, p. 170). This carping over misinterpretation occurs with some frequency, and is perhaps something of an artifice on the part of the author. Nearly everyone prefers reading about vice rather than virtue, but Mateo Alemán continually chides the reader for that preference. The reader is not allowed to view the picaresque experiences from a pedestal or consider himself superior to Guzmán. Both the reader and Guzmán frequently forget the lessons of Christian doctrine and are duly reminded of their negligence.

In effect, the reader is alternately entertained and scolded, enticed into enjoyment and then preached to, so that both the warning and the pleasure are the more vivid.[22] A conflictive relationship exists between the *conseja* and the *consejo* precisely because the *conseja* provides a negative example which tries and tests the value of the *consejo* rather than proving its applicability. The narrative material is inimical to moral teaching. The relationship established between Guzmán and the reader is likewise antagonistic.

The Hypothetical Reader(s) and the Real Reader

The curious narrative technique of anticipating the hypothetical reader's negative response to the work has other effects on the real reader's reaction which are less predictable and more difficult to enunciate. The role of critical reader is a very powerful response-inviting structure (see Chap. I, p. 15) which almost usurps the real reader's spontaneous response to the narration. By way of contrast, the role of Vuestra Merced in *Lazarillo* offers a more distant perspective for the reader to evaluate in that he is a separate identifiable fictional character. In a similar way, the real reader may distance himself from the alien groups of readers addressed in *Guzmán* — the merchants, women, the rich, and so on — whereas the hypothetical reader addressed as «tú» is altogether pervasive. Individual readers naturally differ in their reactions, and each reader must decide whether or not he concurs with the hypothetical critical attitude potentially ascribed to him. The role is insistently indicated for him, but may be resisted, and is only one element in the author's attempt to manipulate reader reaction. In many ways, Guzmán is a good self-critic and well aware of his faults as narrator and their potential to annoy the reader. On further perusal, what may strike the reader with considerable force is that Mateo Alemán has deliberately created a *pícaro*-narrator who is neither altogether likeable nor particularly reliable, since he is both prone to long-winded digressions and unable to practice the doctrine he preaches. His unreliability is communi-

---

[22] ANGEL SAN MIGUEL: *Sentido y Estructura,* p. 67.

cated by the hypothetical reader's response to him. Thus, there is a measure of ironic distance between author and narrator, and the unique or dogmatic perspective of the *pícaro* is relativized by its lack of credibility.[23]

Another possibility is that Guzmán replaces or substitutes the reader's negative reaction with his imagined one, thereby preempting his potential objections before they occur to him. He thus undermines the opposition. The result may be that the reader is left with a more positive and sympathetic response to the narrator. The process of dialectic entices one to entertain the opposing view. The reader may politely protest that he does enjoy the work, sermons and all. The popularity of the work with the contemporary reading public would support this view.

Another effect of the narrator's sensitivity to reader response is to draw the reader emotionally into the narrative. The narrator and reader stay in close contact. The narrator's reaction to the reader is direct and immediate. Furthermore, Guzmán often remarks upon his common humanity and bond with the reader, and his willingness to suffer, Christ-like, in his place. Everything is shared, explained, justified, and confessed to the reader. All is apparently revealed; nothing remains hidden.

In the face of this veritable bombardment, the real reader must at some point retreat to reflect upon and attempt to relate the various contradictory elements of the work to the whole — what Todorov termed the relations «in presentia». Upon doing so, he may still sense an unresolved quality about the work due to what might be called its oxymoronic configuration. Some readers have felt that the work's conflicts are settled in the final conversion of Guzmán and explained by the presence of two narrating personae throughout the work — youthful sinful Guzmanillo and the repentant galley slave, Guzmán.[24] I cannot myself agree with this interpretation, because most of the narrating is undertaken by a supposedly repentant Guzmán, whose attitudes differ very little from those of Guzmanillo, except when he is spewing forth dogma. I suspect that the feature which most unifies the work is the contradictory, yet amazingly consistent, character of Guzmán, a man in many ways at war with himself.[25]

Guzmán's Character and World View and the Reader

The reader cannot fail to be impressed by certain unusual aspects of Guzmán's life experience and character. Guzmán is suspicious, hostile, ineffective as a reformer, and vindictive. Even as an allegedly repentant

[23] BENITO BRANCAFORTE in *Guzmán de Alfarache: ¿Conversión o proceso de degradación?* (Madison: The Hispanic Seminar of Medieval Studies, 1980), pp. 150 ff., develops an interesting analysis of the conflict between the implied author and the narrator. He recognizes the importance of the role of the reader in discerning the irony with which the narrator is treated, but does not include the role of the hypothetical reader in his discussion.

[24] ALEXANDER PARKER: *Literature and the Delinquent* (Edinburgh: The University Press, 1967), p. 44.

[25] BRANCAFORTE: *Guzmán*, pp. 139-161, defines Guzmán's dual personality as that of a *juez-penitente*, and also stresses the insincerity of his conversion; see also the interesting discussion of ARIAS: *The Unrepentant Narrator*, pp. 47, 88-95.

narrator, he in no way exemplifies the virtues he recommends. His actions belie his words and make them suspect. The reader is led to conclude that this is the confession of a liar. Guzmán as a narrator is not to be trusted, yet his heritage and life's experience determine this for him. If he is a dissembler, it is out of necessity rather than choice. The Christian or moral doctrine expounded and the expressed interest in reform do little to change the bitter and unfair world which Guzmán inhabits. Guzmán's view of this world is confirmed by his experience as a *pícaro*. The animal metaphors which abound in his descriptions are expressive of the hostile and suspicious human relationships that prevail. Consider the following:

> Halléme como perro flaco ladrado de los otros, que a todos enseña dientes, todos lo cercan, y acometiendo a todos a ninguno muerde. (II, p. 9)

For Guzmán, even effective revenge is not possible. Any attempt at bettering this world or one's self in it ultimately ends in failure. Dreams are unfulfilled:

> Fueron castillos en arena, fantásticas quimeras. Apenas me vestí que todo estaba en tierra. Tenía trazadas muchas cosas, ninguna salió cierta; antes al revés y de todo punto contraria. Todo fue vano, todo mentira, todo ilusión, todo falso y engaño de la imaginación, todo cisco y carbón, como tesoro de duende. (II, p. 14)

This passage expresses the feeling of defeat and humiliation that follows a typical picaresque experience, producing an attitude of *desengaño* and a sense of frustration. Thus the frequently remarked Sisyphus rhythm of the work — efforts at betterment ending in repeated failures. The resulting pessimism and frustration may also capture the experience of being a *converso* in seventeenth-century Spain.

Guzmán makes frequent complaints about the state of the world, but as a rule then states the reasons why reform is impossible.[26] Guzmán is too fearful, mistrustful, and underconfident to be an effective reformer. Neither conventional wisdom nor Christian dogma succeed in teaching Guzmán how to live well in such a world or how to change it. Thus he remains its victim.

The impossibility of Guzmán's taking effective action may account for the predominant theme of vengeance in the work. The motif surfaces repeatedly. Throughout most of the work Guzmán is obsessed with avenging himself on whomever has most recently mistreated him. His desire for revenge is first evoked by the innkeeper who served him rotten eggs. The punishment he imagines is excessive to say the least. He fantasizes the burning of the woman and her inn, and then and later envisions her hanging by the heels from a tree, having suffered a thousand lashes and been left for dead (I, p. 123).

Early in the narration, two clerics whom Guzmán meets on the road respond to his expressed desire for revenge with a long sermon (I, pp. 126-133). Although Guzmán agrees with them that revenge is vile, he maintains

---

[26] JOHNSON: *Inside Guzmán*, p. 95.

his vindictive mood throughout the work, or, at times, ineffectually pursues revenge. In the guise of Don Juan de Guzmán, he takes vengeance on the Genoese relatives who had treated him so cruelly. Having failed to recover his stolen property in Bologna through legal proceedings, he construes the ensuing litigation as an unsuccessful attempt at vengeance — surely a mis-reading and misuse of a system of justice: «Cuando tu contrario te hiciere injuria, sólo uno te la hace y sólo él compasas; empero por cualquier ca-mino que trates de vengarla, saltaste de la sartén al fuego.» [27] Guzmán successfully avenges himself on Dómine Nicolao, who beat him for stealing preserves from the Cardinal's palace; he retaliates by causing him to be badly bitten by mosquitos (II, p. 259). There are numerous other examples.

Not only is the protagonist vindictive, but so too is the author himself. Mateo Alemán exacts literary revenge on his rival, the imposter Mateo Luján de Sayavedra, who stole his work, by introducing a fictional *pícaro* named Sayavedra into his tale. Sayavedra goes mad and commits suicide, confessing as he leaps over the side of the ship his inferiority to Guzmán as a *pícaro*: «Yo soy la sombra de Guzmán» (IV, p. 141). Some of the intercalated tales, which are not narrated by Guzmán, also treat the theme of vengeance, notably the ghastly tale of «Clorinia y Dorido», and more indirectly the story of «Bonifacio y Dorotea.» The world of the Italian or Byzantine *novella,* replete with beautiful and idealized men and women, sometimes parallels the violence and vengeance present in the picaresque narration. Thus, both the author and his protagonist display a predilection for the theme of vengeance.

Guzmán and the Seventeenth Century Reader

The intensity and lack of detachment in Guzmán's relationship to the reader and the dialogical configuration of the work as a whole have the effect of making *Guzmán de Alfarache* hermetic. The «intratextual» rela-tionships demand the reader's attention. In spite of the variety of the sources, and the polemical quality of some of them,[28] the intensity of the reading experience and the dramatic quality of so many conflicting and contradictory elements in close contact make the relationships «in extensia» less conspicuous than in many other works. *Lazarillo,* in contrast, seems to have been composed as a novelty in dialogue with other contemporary genres, inclining the reader to make comparisons. *Guzmán de Alfarache* combines the tale of the life of a *pícaro,* greatly amplified and more com-plex than that of its prototype *Lazarillo,* with the moral teachings of the

---

[27] Quoted in JOHNSON: *Inside Guzmán,* p. 25; for a more complete discussion of the theme of vengeance in the work than would be appropriate in this chapter, see JOHNSON, pp. 73-84. M. N. NORVAL in «Original Sin and the 'Conversión' in *Guz-mán de Alfarache*», BHS, LI (1974), pp. 352-356, maintains that the episodes of re-venge in the work are opposed to recurring conversions on the part of Guzmán. Guzmán repeatedly succumbs to his passion and then repents. Therefore the final conversion may be regarded as another in a long series and cannot be accepted as likely to last.

[28] CARROLL JOHNSON: «Mateo Alemán y sus fuentes literarias», NRFH, 28 (1979), 360-374.

typical baroque compendium, such as the *silva, floresta, speculum,* or *espejo.* The novelty of *Guzmán,* in the context of the latter, was to provide a unified life story by way of example. The *conseja* usually consisted of various unconnected anecdotes.

Thus it is likely that the contemporary reader would have displayed tremendous delight and vicarious pleasure in the adventures, yet in no way would have expected the purpose of the work to have been other than moral, accustomed as they were to reading miscellanies of doctrinal teachings. Edmond Cros in the third chapter of *Protée et le Gueux,* «Le Premier Public,» discusses contemporary reactions to Guzmán, many to be found in the commentaries of his translators, as well as in the laudatory prologues published with the text of *Guzmán de Alfarache* in Spain.[29] According to Cros, the work was regarded as a mirror in which the reader could see his own vices reflected so that he himself might seek virtue. The English translator, James Mabbe, phrased it thus in one of the accompanying prologues to the translation:

> So an old Bawdes face, Chastness doth suggest:
> vices true picture makes us vice detest
> more than grave Platoes wish; for vertues sight
> can less allure than villany affright.[30]

Cros concludes that Mateo Alemán was primarily admired as a rhetorician, and that Guzmán was regarded as a new miscellaneous collection of anecdotes or *silva.* For his eloquence, Mateo Alemán was known as the *divino español.* Contemporary readers were indifferent to what we regard as the principal narrative structure of *Guzmán.* They were content to interpret the exemplary significance of a rogue's conduct in rhetorical terms, as the amplification of a contrary, and did not seek to reconcile doctrine and narrative in Guzmán's final conversion. Rather, they related doctrine and narrative as they were instructed to in the prologue; the story served as a negative illustration to warn the reader to heed a body of advice that had been somewhat randomly assembled. This collection of doctrinal writings provided whatever shape, structure, or unity there was to the text; the narrative was of secondary importance.

Thus, the contradictions between narrative material and doctrine were probably not particularly bothersome to contemporary readers. Some modern interpreters, assuming the most important portion of the work to be the autobiography of Guzmán, converse with novels and predisposed to accept the aesthetic criterion that a work of art should demonstrate organic unity, have attempted to reconcile these opposing factors to arrive at the meaning of *Guzmán.* They search for signs of Guzmán's development and view the ending or Guzmán's conversion in the galley as the event that bestows meaning on the whole narration. But in reality Guzmán's life and Christian doctrine are not supposed to be reconciled; rather, they are meant to illustrate the great gulf that exists between sin and salvation and

---

[29] EDMOND CROS: *Protée et le Gueux* (Paris: Didier, 1967), pp. 86-128.
[30] Quoted by CROS: *Protée,* p. 98, note 51.

to retain their opposition. The structure of the work is static, and there is
no reason to suppose that Guzmán should change and develop like the hero
of a modern novel. Thus reader expectations, formed and pre-conditioned
by familiarity with the conventions of contemporary literature, affect and
even form the basis for interpretation.

Contemporary readers may also have viewed the final conversion in a
somewhat different light than do modern commentators, many of whom
have been troubled by the question of the conversion's sincerity. The
attitude of the supposedly repentant Guzmán as he narrates his life is
often cynical and bitter. He is motivated by self-interest and various un-
christian passions. Throughout the narration, Guzmán repeatedly repents,
vacillates, and then indulges in his vices, particularly the lust for revenge.
The view of human nature commonly held in Spain during the Counter Re-
formation, based on the doctrine of original sin, does not make Guzmán's
behavior particularly surprising, since the stated purpose of the work is to
provide the example of an evil life so that the reader may live better. In any
case, the reader has also been informed that Guzmán has been condemned
to the galleys, so he expects Guzmán to lead a life of vice. Both the model
of the sinner/saint and the unrepentant sinner were common to Baroque literature with its preference for the graphic representation of dramatic and
unreconciled opposites to test and illustrate theological doctrine.[31] Whether
or not Guzmán's conversions were genuine or lasting, his salvation always
remains a possibility.

Guzmán as the Portrait of a «Converso» and the Reader

What *Guzmán de Alfarache* brings as an innovation to literary representation is the graphic portrayal of a *converso* trying to act as a Christian in a
Christian society. Guzmán is not just a sinner, but a man of little faith, bitter,
cynical, frustrated, and despairing. His *Weltanschauung* and sense of divine
and human retribution are based on the stern Old Testament religion of the
Prophets.[32] The vengeful justice of a wrathful God is more in keeping with
Guzmán's thinking than the merciful forgiveness of Jesus. Guzmán's ostentatious show of religiosity is much like his father's, and, because of his *converso* origins and the general tone of the work, may have been regarded by
readers with suspicion. As Johnson pointed out, *conversos* were always suspect, damned if they appeared too religious and damned if they did not.[33]
On one level, Guzmán may have been interpreted by contemporaries as insincere in his religious convictions, a non-believer from beginning to end, and

---

[31] Examples of sinner/saints are probably more frequent and appear, for instance,
in the following works: LOPE's *La Fianza Satisfecha*, MIRA DE AMESCUA's *El Esclavo
del Demonio*, and MALÓN DE CHAIDE's *La Conversión de la Magdalena*. In TIRSO's
Burlador de Sevilla Don Juan repents too late and dies a sinner. Paulo, in TIRSO's
El Condenado por Desconfiado, might be called a saint/sinner, given his unhappy
end.
[32] NORVAL: «Original Sin», pp. 357-364.
[33] JOHNSON: *Inside Guzmán*, p. 166.

his *discursos* as mere attempts at conforming to the Christian society he had to live in. This possibility makes him an even more interesting and provocative negative example to pose against religious doctrine than otherwise. This would mean that Mateo Alemán, likely a *converso* himself,[34] would have capitalized on his intimate knowledge of *converso* attitudes to create an orthodox miscellany of doctrine, using a heterodox character to both exemplify vice and to narrate.

The way that the reader is invited to participate in the work, in the light of a *converso* protagonist, is also telling. To recapitulate: the reader addressed in the prologue as the preferred reader of the text is a wise and discreet reader, interested in moral doctrine, who understands how to interpret the evil antics of the *pícaro* — as a warning to himself and not as a life to be imitated. Ignorant readers, like the *vulgo*, will ignore the work's moral teaching and relish the tale of the *pícaro*'s life. However, the ideal discreet reader is seldom the reader addressed in the main body of the narration. Guzmán flatters the reader at first and berates himself. He apologetically and obsequiously begins his account of his parents' life and then his own. Later it is the hypothetical reader who errs, like the *vulgo*, by showing more interest in the *pícaro*'s bad example than in moral doctrine. The hypothetical reader, the reader Guzmán most often addressed and anticipated as the potential reader of his test, is unable to live up to the standards of the ideal reader, just as Guzmán is not able to live as a perfect man. Throughout the work the ideal is opposed to the real and the enormous gulf between them is emphasized. Some of the text's structures invite the reader to regard himself as a kindred spirit of Guzmán, in effect to identify with a *converso*.

The reader, mortal and a sinner, inhabits the same real world as Guzmán. Some of his foibles are to criticize Guzmán's sermonizing, to prefer fable, to question the reliability of the *pícaro*-narrator as preacher, and to argue with Guzmán. Through the ensuing dialogues the work progresses, and the reader and the *pícaro* learn, although they may not practice what is preached. The reader is mortal like Guzmán, but he is also Guzmán's critic. Therefore, Guzmán fears him as he fears the world. Guzmán's approach to the reader is consistent with his approach to the world — emotional and suspicious. The reader is implicated in the hostile world of enemies that Guzmán perceives, where men and animals regard one another with mistrust and even hatred:

> Todo anda revuelto, todo apriesa, todo marañado. No hallarás hombre con hombre; todos vivimos en asechanza los unos de los otros, como el gato para el ratón o la araña para la culebra, que hallándola descuidada, se deja colgar de un hilo y, asiéndola de la cerviz, la aprieta fuertemente, no apartándose della hasta que con su ponzoña la mata. (II, p. 54)

---

[34] PETER DUNN in *The Spanish Picaresque Novel*, p. 41 and p. 148, notes the lack of documentary proof for Alemán's *converso* origin.

Guzmán's fear of persecution, defensive attitude, and obsession with the theme of vengeance indicate that he is discontented and angry. The suppressed aggression of the narrator is readily and directly communicated to the reader, both by the tone of the work and in the way the reader is approached. *Guzmán de Alfarache* is thus one of the most discomforting works of fiction ever produced.

CHAPTER IV

THE READER AND HOMOLOGOUS STRUCTURES
IN *EL BUSCON*

The early years of the Seventeenth Century witnessed the publication of a plethora of works of fiction, following the appearance of the *Primera Parte* of *Guzmán de Alfarache* in 1599. *Guzmán* and also *Lazarillo* are fundamental to the evolution of early seventeenth-century narrative fiction. The *Pícara Justina*, the apocryphal *Guzmán*, the first part of the *Quijote*, the second part of Alemán's *Guzmán*, and *El Buscón* are all believed to have been composed between 1600 and 1605. Some critics consider *Guzmán* the archetypal picaresque text and model which most influenced the others;[1] but whatever the case, all are episodic pseudo-autobiographies of *pícaros,* with the exception of the *Quijote,* which contains a playfully ironic comment on picaresque narrative in the episode of Ginés de Pasamonte.

The use of an intertextual approach seems particularly appropriate in analyzing the aforementioned works. However, within this context the methods I have utilized vary somewhat. The intertextual relationships explored in *Lazarillo* included a number of texts that were not literary and also took into account *Lazarillo*'s negative response to various contemporary genres of fiction. On the other hand, *Guzmán* developed in dialogue with the anticipated response of the reader. The contradictory nature of the protagonist and the tension implicit between what was practiced and what was preached induce the reader to respond more readily to the intratextual relationships. *Guzmán* is a work whose intensity captivates the reader in an emotional web, and prevents his escape from its labyrinthine meanderings to ponder matters extrinsic to the text. In the treatment of the *Buscón,* my use of an intertextual approach will primarily focus on the

---

[1] SAYAVEDRA's apocryphal *Guzmán* was published in 1602. The first version of *El Buscón* is thought to have been composed in 1603 and 1604 (see the critical edition of Lázaro Carreter cited below, p. XIV), although the work was not published until 1626. *La Pícara Justina* was first published in 1605. *Guzmán* is widely regarded as the central or pivotal work of the genre. See, for example, A. A. PARKER: *Literature and the Delinquent* (Edinburgh: Edinburgh University Press, 1967), pp. 33-36; CARLOS BLANCO AGUINAGA: «Cervantes y la Picaresca...», pp. 313-328. For a contrary opinion, see PETER DUNN: «Problems of a model for the picaresque», pp. 96-97; GUILLÉN, in *Literature as System,* pp. 72-74, stresses the influence of both *Lazarillo* and *Guzmán.*

influence of *Guzmán* and *Lazarillo*. My assumption is that the *Buscón* was partly composed in answer to those works, and perhaps others, and constituted a new variation on the picaresque theme. Many echoes of *Lazarillo* and *Guzmán* can be detected in *El Buscón*, although their function and significance may differ radically in this new context. A study of these reminiscences serves as a heuristic device whereby some salient characteristics of the *Buscón* may be better clarified. The technique would be equally applicable to the works of other writers of the period, such as Cervantes, since his ironic treatment of the picaresque includes many specific references and allusions to those preexisting texts. The scope of this study, then, narrows as it progresses. More will be said about literary conventions than extra-literary texts.

As in the chapters on *Lazarillo* and *Guzmán*, I begin with an examination of the roles of the reader indicated in the prologues. Here the inherent duality in the work's aesthetic purpose is linked to a divergence in reader response. The function and character of the fictitious reader in the main body of the text and *El Buscón*'s imitations of and departures from its predecessors, *Lazarillo* and *Guzmán*, are next described. A negative reaction to past literary models and contemporary society results in literary parody and social satire being important principles of the work. The same destructive inclination, the tendency to undercut or undermine his original statements or point of departure, is evidenced in the figuration of the prose, the treatment of objective reality and of the Buscón himself, and even in the development of the fictitious reader's role. Quevedo's treatment of the reader is thus consistent with other aspects of his art. At the same time, the resulting network of negativities evokes an ambiguous and contradictory response from the real reader.

The Prologue

Some ways in which *El Buscón* responds to and also departs from some of the canons adhered to by *Lazarillo* and *Guzmán* are evident in the various dedications of the prologue. It is likely that not all of these were written by Quevedo himself, but rather by his book dealer Roberto Duport.[2] Nonetheless, they are useful in indicating the purposes of the author in composing the work, as well as how the work was most likely interpreted by contemporary readers; they provide the same sort of information as the laudatory prologues at the beginning of *Guzmán*. In the petition for a publication license addressed to the king, the epithets ascribed to the work, «exemplo de vagabundos y espejo de tacaños» (p. 4), suggest that it was meant to serve as a mirror in which the reader might see his own folly exposed. Later the work is described as «emulo de Guzmán de Alfarache (y aun no se si diga mayor) y tan agudo y gracioso como Don Quijote» (p. 6). The work patently imitates many of the characteristics

---

[2] FERNANDO LÁZARO CARRETER: «Introducción y edición crítica de *La Vida del Buscón llamado Pablos*» (Salamanca: Consejo Superior de Investigaciones Científicas, 1965), p. XV, note 6, and p. LXXVIII. All further references to *El Buscón* are from this edition and will be cited in the text of the book itself.

and the form of *Guzmán*, and even exaggerates them, but is both wittier and more humorous than *Guzmán*. The comic purpose of the work is several times alluded to in the prologue «Al lector». The reader is expected to find Pablos amusing and to be entertained by his picaresque deceits:

> Qve desseoso te considero Lector, o oydor (que los ciegos no pueden leer) de registrar lo gracioso de don Pablos Principe de la vida Buscona. Aqui hallaras en todo genero de Picardia (de que pienso que los mas gustan) sutilezas, engaños, inuenciones, y modos, nacidos del ocio para viuir a la droga... (p. 7)

The moral purpose of the work is next stated, but also minimized. The reader is informed that he can learn from the «escarmiento», i.e., that he should be warned by the experiences of the *pícaro* not to repeat them in his own life. If he does not pay attention to the lessons implicit in the *pícaro*'s mistakes, he may at least derive some advantage from the sermons contained in the work. But the efficacy of the work's moral purpose is undermined by the reader's assumed disinterest. The narrator of the prologue doubts that any reader buys a book of jests in order to reform his depraved nature. Therefore, the reader is in effect invited to interpret the work as he wishes, but at the same time to give it well-deserved praise. When he laughs at the work's quips and jokes («when» not «if»), the reader is expected to praise the work and its author, who has savvy enough to know that the life of a *pícaro* is more amusing than are fictions of a more serious nature:

> ... y no poco fruto podras sacar del si tienes atencion al escarmiento; y quando no la hagas, aprouechate de los sermones, que dudo nadie compre libro de burlas para apartarse de los incentivos de su natural deprauado. Sea empero lo que quisieres, dale aplauso, que bien lo merece, y quando te rias de sus chistes, alaba el ingenio de quien sabe conocer que tiene mas deleyte, saber vidas de Picaros, descritas con gallardia, que otras inuenciones de mayor ponderacion. (p. 7)

There is no disapproval expressed of the reader's desire to be amused. Rather, he is free to ponder the lessons or sermons if he wishes, or to laugh unencumbered by the remembrance of more serious matters. According to the interpretation advanced in this prologue, Quevedo's approach to the reader is ostensibly to delight rather than to teach, and offers a contrast to the admonishments and conditions posited in Mateo Alemán's prologues to the reader («No te rías de la conseja y se te pase el consejo» (*Guzmán* I, p. 34)). Moreover, there are virtually no long moralizing digressions in the *Buscón*. Whatever message there is must be extracted from the narrative and the brief commentary provided by the protagonist or other characters. The moral purpose of the *Buscón*, although mentioned in the prologue, is consistently refuted and ignored throughout the work.

Finally the preface broaches the subject of commercial success. (*Guzmán* was surely worthy of emulation in this respect.) The hope is expressed that the reader has bought the book, not just browsed through it in the bookshop. In the latter case he is a freeloader (*gorrón*), and will misinterpret the work because he will read it piecemeal. In effect, the reader is accused of misreading and miserliness, and shamed and goaded into buying the book:

> Su Autor, ya le sabes, el precio del libro no le ignoras, pues ya le tienes en tu casa, sino es que en la del Librero le hojeas, cosa pesada para el, y que se auia de quitar con mucho rigor, que ay gorrones de libros, come de almuerços; y hombre que saca cuento leyendo a pedaços, y en diuersas vezes, y luego le zurze; y es gran lastima que tal se haga, porque este mormura sin costarle dineros, poltroneria vastarda, y miseria no hallada del Cauallero de la Tenaza. Dios te guarde de mal libro, de Alguaziles, y de muger rubia, pedigueña y cariredonda. (p. 7)

By this persuasive subterfuge, a paying readership is solicited, and the bookshop browser is discouraged. The latter will misrepresent the work, combining its truths in the form of a lie (*zurcir*), and exhibits a laziness and stinginess not to be found in the Buscón himself. The reader's propensity for picaresque pleasures is coyly implied by the final ironic benediction — that God keep him safe from policemen and conniving women. The intended reader then, to whom the author addresses his narration, is characterized by a love of wit, the potential to be something of a *pícaro*, and a lack of interest in moral doctrine.

It should be reiterated at this point that Quevedo's authorship of the prologue «Al lector» is doubtful (see note 2), since it is not included in Manuscripts C and S, but only in E, published by the book dealer Roberto Duport in 1626. Duport frequently tampered with Quevedo's manuscripts, and it may be supposed that «al lector» is one of his additions to Quevedo's text. A book dealer's interest in the work's commercial possibilities is evident in the passage, as well as an awareness of what makes books sell — seldom their moralizing. What is perhaps interesting is that Duport, as a contemporary reader, is given credence by some modern critics who, perhaps influenced by his interpretation, stress Quevedo's skill as a humorist and the reader's interest in the *pícaro*'s japes and other antics. I have considered his instructions to the reader perspicacious enough to base some of my interpretation on this early reading of the work. The «Carta Dedicatoria» of the prologue, on the other hand, is almost certainly by Quevedo, since it appears in Manuscripts C and S, which were not edited by Duport.

Echoing *Lazarillo,* Quevedo includes in *El Buscón* a vaguely defined fictitious reader know only as «vuestra merced», first mentioned in the brief «Carta Dedicatoria» that precedes the narration. Here the fictitious narrator, Pablos, addresses the fictitious reader, vuestra merced, having heard that vuestra merced has expressed a desire to hear or understand the various discourses of this life.

> Habiendo sabido el deseo que v.m. tiene de entender los varios discursos de mi vida, por no dar lugar a que otro (como en ajenos casos) mienta, he querido enviarle esta relación, que no le será pequeño alivio para los ratos tristes. Y porque pienso ser largo en contar cuán corto he sido de ventura, dejaré de serlo ahora. (p. 11)

The commonplace eager and curious reader is predicated then, and the purpose of entertainment is reiterated in a new way. The *Buscón* is supposed to provide the reader relief from the doldrums. The narrator then alludes to his own propensity for bad luck, thus foreshadowing the tone of the account. Paradoxically, the tale of another's misfortunes is expected to alleviate the reader's moments of sadness. Two truisms about the effect of fiction on the reader are implied in this passage: that it offers escape from one's own life and that reading about another's misery provides solace. No mention is made in the «Carta Dedicatoria» of deceit, tricks, wit, conceits, or humor, perhaps a significant omission. Rather the fictitious narrator's expressed purpose is serious — to communicate the truth to v.m. about his life. Pablos, «not wanting to give anyone else the opportunity to lie about him,» sends v.m. the «relación» of his life. This passage might and it is difficult to discount this possibility since the term «relación» in Golden Age letters often referred to historical accounts written to support particular interests. Nonetheless, the wording is somewhat ambiguous. V. m.'s desire to hear the «varios discursos» is puzzling. The implication is, I believe, that v.m. has heard of Pablos and various tales about him and, having been amused, hopes to hear more. In the body of the text Pablos oc- be interpreted ironically to mean that Pablos prefers to tell his own lie, casionally refers to the fame of his escapades. For example, «... hasta hoy no se ha acabado de solemnizar la burla en Alcalá» (p. 88), and «Con estas y otras cosas, comencé a cobrar fama de travieso y agudo entre todos» (p. 89).[3]

The Nature of «Buscón»'s Duality

The generic duality of *El Buscón*, giving rise to two common and highly diverse interpretations of the work, is already indicated in the prologue. On the one hand the work is a pseudo-autobiography, the tale of someone who suffers misfortune, becomes a *pícaro*, and explains his life story to v.m. On the other hand, it is a book of jests, the *tour de force* of a stylist, the author-in-the-text, freely indulging his preference for witticisms, puns, conceits, and other examples of verbal artifice meant to amuse the reader-in-the-text. Like *Guzmán*, the work has a hybrid quality. The story of Guzmán's life is laced with moralizing digressions, whereas *El Buscón* is decorated with a startling display of verbal ingenuity and black humor. The resulting inconsistencies in tone and matter must be responsible for the divided critical response the work has engendered.[4] In a recent article, Edwin Williamson states the problem thus:

[3] For a somewhat different interpretation of the «Carta Dedicatoria» see GON-ZALO DÍAZ MIGOYO: *Estructura de la Novela. Anatomía de El Buscón* (Madrid: Editorial Fundamentos, 1978), pp. 72-78; pp. 138-141.

[4] Some character-centered readings of *El Buscón* are to be found in A. A. PARKER: *Literature and the Delinquent*, pp. 56-71; A. I. BAGBY: «The Conventional Golden Age *Pícaro* and Quevedo's Criminal *Pícaro*», *KRQ*, 14 (1967), 311-319; T. E. MAY: «Good and Evil in the *Buscón*: A Survey», *MLR*, 45 (1950), 319-335; RICHARD BJORNSON: «Moral Blindness in Quevedo's *El Buscón*», *RR*, 67 (1976), 50-59; and PETER N. DUNN: «El individuo y la sociedad en *La Vida del Buscón*», *BH*, 52 (1950), 375-

There are those who wish to understand the book as a coherent moral vision of a corrupt society, expressed through the point of view of a criminal individual, and others who reject any serious moral concern in the novel and see it as an arrogant display of black humor directed against an inferior and despised social class.[5]

A number of more recent articles and books have attempted to synthesize these variant interpretations,[6] and point out, correctly in my opinion, that an adequate appreciation of the work's significance must derive from a consideration of the whole and not just from an examination of one or another of its aspects. Yet the work elicits a divided and complex response from its readers and is built on that tension. A consideration of Quevedo's approach to the reader, in conjunction with other elements of the work, indicates some of the ways in which a holistic interpretation of the work may be arrived at and clarifies the nature of its ambiguity. The image or images of the reader created in the prologues indicate two perspectives from which the work can be and has been viewed. The two interpretations may have arisen because readers, naturally expecting to be oriented in the prologue, heeded Duport's advice; or, they may be implicit in the character of the text itself. The nature of this dual aesthetic purpose can be schematized as follows, the elements under consideration being the narrator, the narration, and the reader:

| Author in text | Book of jests | Reader in text |
| Fictitious narrator (Pablos) | Life of a *pícaro* | Fictitious reader (v. m.) |

The possible differences in aesthetic purpose and attitude between the author-in-the-text and the fictitious narrator are obscured in the main body of the narration because the autobiography in its entirety is narrated by Pablos. In effect, he recounts his life in a humorous way, and the author's voice is subsumed in the voice of the fictitious narrator. The dichotomy posited between the style of the work and the tale of the *pícaro*'s life, between the textual and the generic, is unified in the persona of the *pícaro*.

396. Stylistic analyses of *El Buscón* predominate in FERNANDO LÁZARO CARRETER: «Originalidad del *Buscón*», *Estilo barroco y personalidad creadora* (Salamanca: Anaya, 1966), pp. 109-141, and «Glosas críticas a *Los Pícaros en la Literatura* de A. A. Parker», *HR*, 41 (1973), 469-497; RAIMUNDO LIDA: «Estilística. Un estudio sobre Quevedo», *Sur*, 4 (1931), 163-172; «Sobre el arte verbal del *Buscón*», *Philological Quarterly*, 51, No. 1 (1972), pp. 255-269; and «Pablos de Segovia y su agudeza», *Homenaje a Casalduero* (Madrid: Editorial Gredos, 1972), pp. 258-298; LEO SPITZER: *L'art de Quevedo dans le Buscón*, trans. by M. and Mme. Dauer (Paris: Ediciones Hispanoamericanas, 1972).

[5] EDWIN WILLIAMSON: «The Conflict between Author and Protagonist in Quevedo's *Buscón*», *Journal of Hispanic Philology*, 2 (1977), 45.

[6] See, for example, EDWIN WILLIAMSON: «Conflict...», pp. 45-60; WILLIAM H. CLAMURRO: «The Destabilized Sign: Word and Form in Quevedo's *Buscón*», *MLN*, vol. 95, No. 2 (March, 1980), pp. 295-311; GONZALO DÍAZ MIGOYO: *Estructura...*, esp. pp. 10-12; RAIMUNDO LIDA: «Pablos de Segovia y su agudeza», pp. 258-298; JAMES IFFLAND: «Pablos' Voice: His Master's? A Freudian Approach to Wit in *El Buscón*», *RF*, 91 (1979), 215-243.

The emphasis that Williamson and others have given to the problem of the work's serious moral vision, or lack of it, perhaps obscures the issue, as does the assumption that Pablos is victimized by Quevedo's humor, that the jokes are Quevedo's and the life is Pablos'. For Pablos functions in two ways in the narration: first as an observer, the vehicle and voice of the satire; second as the actor or «liver» of a life. His dual function is expressed in the following diagram:

Pablos as narrator and observer provides the reader with a satirical vision of the world. The black humor in the work is directed at everyone and everything rather than just at Pablos and the lower class *pícaros*, although aristocrats are generally spared by their very absence from the work.[7] Don Diego Coronel, a member of a wealthy *converso* family, is just as great a *pícaro* in his own way as is Pablos himself.[8] Both are very much products of this world, pragmatism (for better or for worse) their guiding principle. What Pablos thinks and does are results of what he sees, and his pessimistic world view may be understood in relation to the trajectory of his life. The plot of the work, which may be regarded as the *pícaro*'s life story, is economic, well-wrought, and clear in its progress. Pablos' repeated failures to better himself in the world may be considered the author's answer to what might happen to a criminal individual who aspires to be a gentleman. In turn, Pablos' satirical vision of the world and black humor may be interpreted as defensive reactions to the hardships endured. The reader sympathizes with the hardships and, with Pablos, distances the pain with laughter. The perspective of the protagonist is readily explained by his environment. Seen in this way, the work may be credited with a coherent as opposed to a contradictory essence. Pablos as observer and narrator is the logical extension of Pablos the actant, for he exacts literary vengeance on a world which has mistreated him.

The Function of the Fictitious Reader, V.M.

In the tradition of *Lazarillo*, Pablos periodically addresses a fictitious reader in the body of the narration, twice referred to as «señor» in the beginning of the first and second chapters, and most of the rest of the time as «vuestra merced». As mentioned before, vuestra merced is first alluded to in the «Carta Dedicatoria» of the prologue. However, in *El Buscón*, vuestra merced is not at all defined and has no functional significance in the plot. There is no *caso* to explain in *El Buscón*. In *Lazarillo*

[7] GONZALO DÍAZ MIGOYO: *Estructura...*, p. 87, 88.
[8] CARROLL JOHNSON: «El Buscón: D. Pablos, D. Diego, y D. Francisco», *Hispanófila*, 51 (1974), 1-26.

the past is narrated to explain the present. Vuestra Merced's request provides the fictional *raison d'être* of the narration and facilitates its circular structure, since the work begins with mention of the *caso* and ends with more information both about the *caso* and vuestra merced. Vuestra merced is addressed periodically throughout the narrative to stress certain points of importance.

In contrast, Quevedo would seem to use the device of addressing vuestra merced for other purposes. He often utilizes this narrative technique to ease the transition from the picaresque narration to an event introduced because it generates a pun, or for its outrageous or shock effect — that is, to join together just those variant features which have given rise to the diverse interpretations I mentioned before. For it is true that the conceptist style of Quevedo frequently interrupts the plot and exaggerates the qualities of the characters. Mimetic representation is often fragmented, viewed through a distorting lens, and eccentrically restored. The addresses to v.m. prepare the reader for such a change, indicate how he should react, or provide a transition to the new material.

The first example of this occurs when, at Don Diego's instigation, Pablos taunts the *converso* Poncio de Aguirre by calling him Poncio Pilato. Pablos is so traumatized by the beating that Poncio de Aguirre gives him that he promises never to mention the name of Poncio Pilato again. However, the next day in church he mistakenly substitutes the name of Poncio de Aguirre for Poncio Pilato in reciting the Creed. Quevedo prepares the reader for the incongruity and irreverence of this slip of the tongue by addressing v.m. directly with the following warning: «advierta v.m. la inocente malicia» (p. 25).

The next case in point is the «rey de gallos» episode, during which Pablos postulates that he has been attacked by the vegetable vendors because they mistook him for his mother. His dress for the carnivalesque celebration includes a hat with feathers, recalling that his mother had on occasion been tarred and feathered and driven out of town as a witch. Since Pablos is wearing feathers, he speculates that the vendors may have thereby succumbed to such a delusion. This ludicrous suggestion is included for its humor or surprise effect, as Rico has pointed out,[9] and is introduced by «de paso quiero confesar a v.m.» (p. 29).

Another bizarre incident that Pablos attempts to verify by protesting its truth to v.m. is his description of the *vizcaíno* who had forgotten how to eat. He concretizes the unbelievable by establishing himself as eye-witness to the incident, by identifying the character in question by name and birthplace, by describing the actions of the *vizcaíno* as he attempts to eat, and by swearing to v.m. that what he saw was true:

> Certifico a v.m. que vi a uno dellos, al más flaco, que se llamaba Jurre, vizcaíno, tan olvidado ya de cómo y por dónde se comía que una cortecilla que le cupo la llevó dos veces a los ojos, y entre tres veces no le acertaban a encaminar las manos a la boca. (p. 38)

[9] Francisco Rico: *La Novela Picaresca y el Punto de Vista*, p. 128.

Sometimes Pablos addresses v.m. following an unlikely or preposterous event — as if to insure the reader's continuing presence, willing suspension of disbelief, or participatory reading of the same. Such is the case after Pablos falls off his horse into a dung heap («Púseme cual v.m. puede imaginar» (p. 28)), or after an outlandish meal is served by the schoolmaster Cabra, which includes as its main dish *cabra asada*. A variety of implications and innuendos arise from the dual significance of the word «cabra» as both man and meal. Attention is called to Cabra's name, to its possible association with the insulting label «cabrón», to the possible likeness of Cabra's physique or character to that of the goat, to the fact that an unusual dish of the same name is being eaten by his students, and to a latent image of their eating Cabra himself, i.e., cannibalism. It is perfectly clear that such a meal is served in order to alert the reader to these associations. Pablos somewhat apologetically calls v.m.'s attention to his own quite ludicrous imagination. His comment, «mire v.m. si inventara el diablo tal cosa,» may be interpreted as an admission that this time he has gone too far.

Occasionally Pablos' addresses to v.m. interrupt a thought, as though the narrator had suddenly become aware that the reader might be surprised or shocked by the content of the narration. Some of these occasions involve major decisions or turning points in Pablos' life. For example, after his mistreatment by the other students at the University of Alcalá, he decides to fight fire with fire and to adopt a picaresque ethic to make his way in the world:

> ... vine a resolverme de ser bellaco con los bellacos y más, si pudiese, que todos. No sé si salí con ello, pero yo aseguro a v.m. que hice todas las diligencias posibles. (p. 74)

Pablos' decision to leave the theater and to become a «suitor of nuns» is also interrupted in order to consider the reader's anticipated response:

> ... y yo, que entendí salir de mala vida con no ser farsante, si no lo ha v.m. por enojo, di en amante de red, como cofia, y por hablar más claro, en pretendiente de Anticristo, que es lo mismo que galán de monjas. (p. 264)

The structure of the passage just cited is relatively common in the prose of Quevedo both in the *Buscón* and in other works as well. Suspense is built up by warning the reader of his possible reaction and by mystifying him with a series of enigmatic jokes and initially incomprehensible metaphors. There follows a resolution or «demystification»,[10] in which the reader is enlightened as to the true meaning of the images; in this passage it is at last clearly stated that Pablos became a «galán de monjas», explaining the prior epithets «amante de red» and «pretendiente de Anticristo.»

Another address to v.m. occurs in the middle of his description of the fantastic dress of Don Toribio, and again calls attention to the bizarre imagination of the narrator manifested here:

---

[10] On the pattern of demystification in the prose of *El Buscón* see EDMOND CROS: *L'Aristocrate et le Carnaval des Gueux. Etude sur le Buscón de Quevedo* (Montpellier: Centre d'Etudes Sociocritiques, 1975).

Quítose la capa y traía —¡mire v.m. quién tal pensara!— la ropilla, de pardo paño la delantera, y la trasera de lienzo blanco, con sus fondos en sudor. (p. 166).

Such asides may be interpreted as acknowledgements that Pablos was aware that his prolific fancy might overwhelm v.m. He interjects exclamatory statements to v.m. to soften the shock and also to connect these flights of fancy with the principal occurrences of the narration of Pablos' life. There are further such instances of addressing v.m. scattered throughout the text which are important, but do not substantially add to the analysis offered here.[11]

Quevedo, through his narrator Pablos, acknowledges the presence of the reader in other ways as well. At times he interjects brief critical comments that demonstrate his consideration of the reader's attention span, patience, and tastes. At the same time the reader is privy to the narrator's strategy in telling his tale. Like Lazarillo, Pablos selects from the fund of material about his life and frequently mentions that he has refrained from recounting a lengthier version or giving more examples. Remarks such as «Y por no ser largo, dejo de contar como hacía...» (p. 88), «Por no cansar a vuestra merced vengo a decir...» (p. 144), or «Pero volvamos a las cosas que el dicho mi tío hacía...» (p. 148) frequently interrupt the sequential narration. Pablos' interest in brevity is coupled with care not to offend the reader with crude or obscene language so that occasionally he precedes the offensive material with apologetic expressions such as «Hablando con perdón» (p. 28 and p. 136), and «si no lo ha v.m. por enojo» (p. 264). Like Lazarillo and Guzmán his demonstrated attitude toward the reader is courteous and deferential, belying to some degree the harsh nature of his tale.

Another technique reminiscent of *Lazarillo* and even more so of *Guzmán* is the inclusion of third person opinion, particularly in recounting the character and infamous deeds of his parents. These temporary lapses in narratorial authority allow Pablos to adopt an attitude of ingenuous innocence in regard to his parents' more suspect activities. The examples are most frequent early in the work:

Dicen que era de muy buena cepa... (p. 15)

Malas lenguas daban en decir que mi padre metía el dos de bastos para sacar el as de oros. (p. 16)

Sólo diz que se dijo no sé qué de un cabrón y volar. (p. 17)

Hubo fama que reedificaba doncellas... (p. 17)

Unos la llamaban zurcidora de gustos... (p. 17)

Pablos also addresses himself in occasional asides commencing with «decía yo entre mí» (p. 36), or «dije entre mí» (p. 73) to make ironic comments or secret decisions. Thus the reader has access to information not available

---

[11] Other examples may be found on p. 37, p. 78, and p. 80. Rhetorical questions serve the same function as addresses to v.m. on p. 87 and p. 97.

to the other characters in the fiction. The reader is made Pablos' confidant, just as he is in *Lazarillo*.

Toward the end of the narration Pablos continues to address the fictitious reader as v.m. in some instances, but also addresses him in various new ways. He directs himself to v.m. after he has found out the true nature of nuns, sensing that the reader will want to hear no more about them: «Y no quiera v.m. saber más de que las Bautistas todas enronquecieron...» (p. 270). He then invites the «pious reader» to consider to what extent the nun's grief after he left her was due to loss of Pablos or loss of what he had stolen from her:

> Lo que la monja hizo de sentimiento, más por lo que la llevaba que por mí, considérelo el pío lector. (p. 271)

The «pious reader's» faith in the church, view of human nature, and assumptions about himself might well be contradicted by Pablos' account of his adventures with the nun. Throughout the narration the piety of both the «pillar of the church» and the «holier than thou» reader, if such there be, is undermined by Pablos' satire and the impossibility of his surviving according to virtuous principles in the world thus satirized. In any case most readers are not pious and to be abruptly addressed as such can be disquieting. The real reader may then consider Pablos' actions against the background of his own piety; the fiction becomes a mirror in which to see himself.

In the final chapter Pablos discusses his success as gambler and card-shark. He claims that the ignorant may learn both tricks and modes of speaking from him so that they are better prepared. Yet those who read his book will be deceived by these same tactics:

> Mas quizá declarando yo algunos chanzas y modos de hablar, estarán avisados los ignorantes, y los que leyeren mi libro serán engañados por su culpa. (p. 273)

Here it seems that alternative and conflicting roles are suggested for the reader, that of an ignorant man who can learn to be a *pícaro* and that of an innocent man who «consents» to be deceived.

Pablos then addresses the hypothetical reader in a variety of ways — as «tú», «hombre», and then «por si fueres pícaro, lector." In effect, the reader is warned to be careful playing cards, whatever his role and with whomever he is playing:

> No te fíes, hombre, en dar tú la baraja, que te la trocarán al depabilar una vela. Guarda el naipe de tocamientos, raspados o bruñidos, cosa con que se conocen los azares. Y por si fueres pícaro, lector, advierte que en cocinas y caballerizas, pican con un alfiler o doblan los azares, para conocerlos por lo hendido. Y si tratares con gente honrada, guárdate del naipe... (p. 273)

This passage is more reminiscent of Guzmán's sermonizing digressions and way of addressing the reader than of Lazarillo's. The voice of the narrator

97

seems closer to that of Quevedo than to Pablos, emerging from the cocoon of the fictional, as it were. The reader is offered a number of optional roles in rapid succession: that of an ignoramus who will learn picaresque talk and tricks, the victim of the *pícaro* who has learned from the text, a man who is being preached to about the dangers of gaming, and an aspiring *pícaro* who is deficient in some of the tricks of the trade. The reader is presented with various potential responses to Pablos' observations on gambling, and moreover, hints as to their practical application. He is no longer treated deferentially as someone of superior social status. The created role of the fictional reader-in-the-text is here withdrawn by posing a variety of new ways in which the reader may relate to the text.

In *El Buscón* Quevedo utilizes the conventions of both *Lazarillo* and *Guzmán* in addressing the reader. However, the technique of addressing v.m. is emptied of its formal or structural significance in the plot and is used more as a way of connecting or anchoring the paradigmatic digressions or humorous outbursts to the contiguous chain of the text. At the same time Quevedo establishes an image of the reader as a man of superior social status and discerning literary tastes, who is socially and morally superior to Pablos and will therefore be shocked by the more sordid aspects of Pablos' life. In the final addresses to v.m., «pío lector», «los que leyeren mi libro», «tú», «hombre», and «por si fueres pícaro, lector», Quevedo abruptly implies that different types of readers might interpret his text in different ways. He records a range of possibilities for the reader to consider and in the process the original role developed for the reader disintegrates. Now the reader is asked to consider where he stands within the context of the picaresque world — as one of the deceivers or one of the deceived. In the text of *El Buscón*, the reader is first respected and set apart from the world satirized, and then summarily thrust into it. As we shall see, the pattern of setting up and then knocking down, or of creating illusions and then destroying them, is fundamental to the structure of the *Buscón*. In general, one might say that Pablos usually imitates the conventions of addressing the reader initiated in *Lazarillo* and, very briefly, emulates those of *Guzmán,* in both cases ignoring the particular functional or structural capacity they served in the earlier texts.[12] Rather, Quevedo puts them to new uses. *Guzmán*'s intense approach to the reader is brought into brief play to demolish the fictitious reader's superiority and distance from the picaresque world.

In the body of the text the image projected of the hypothetical reader is that of one who expects verisimilitude in the narration and will be surprised by, as well as skeptical of, that which he reads. The purpose of addressing him is ostensibly to convince him of the tangibility of the perverse world depicted, but this overt purpose is a pretense, since it is the impact itself of the outrageous or shocking which in part governs and bestows the humor of the work. The addresses to the reader in fact call his attention to this quality of the text and surreptitiously suggest the appropriate response to such material. Judging by my own experience,

---

[12] For slightly different conclusions see EDMOND CROS: *L'Aristocrate...*, pp. 98, 99.

the real reader is indeed caught somewhat off guard by the humor and singular style of the work, and some of the meaning of the work derives from the attendant parodic and satiric structures. Other important features which shape meaning are the figuration of the prose, the structure of the plot, and comparisons with earlier picaresque novels.

Echoes of «Lazarillo» and «Guzmán»

Various elements of previous picaresque novels aside from the conventions of addressing the reader are reelaborated in *El Buscón,* and the reader's recognition of their submerged presence may affect his interpretation of the work. Typological analogues may be found to some of the characters in the work. Cabra recalls the avaricious *clérigo* of Maqueda; Don Toribio resembles the *escudero* of the *Tercer Tratado* of *Lazarillo.* The descriptions of the geneology and parents of the *pícaro* and his venture out into the world at an early age are features common to all picaresque narrations, as is an episodic structure. A series of caricatured persons are encountered on the road by Pablos, as they are by Guzmán. The «Premática del desengaño contra los poetas güeros, chirles y hebenes» in *El Buscón* recalls «las ordenanzas mendicativas» in *Guzmán.* Chapters 2-6 of the *Primera Parte* of the latter, which depict customs and travails of the beggars of Rome, parallel Chapters 5 and 6 of Book II and Chapters 1, 2, and 3 of Book III, wherein Pablos describes the communal life of the *colegio buscón.* Thus, various similarities occur in plot and content both in *El Buscón* and other picaresque works.[13]

Where *El Buscón* differs radically from *Guzmán* is in its aesthetic motive, manifested in its style and approach to the reader. There is implied an utter rejection of the moralizing purpose inherent in *Guzmán.* *El Buscón* has nothing to do with the creation of a perfect man, and does not regard the *pícaro*'s wisdom or vision as an «atalaya de la vida humana». Pablos writes with an attitude of bitter disillusion reflected in his acerbic wit; his perspective is hardly that of a converted soul, even an insincere one. He makes no pretence to repent or reform or even change. Rather he is an obstinate sinner, as he implies at the end of the work when he plans to depart for the New World with the strumpet, la Grajales:

> Y que vi que duraba mucho este negocio y más la fortuna en perseguirme, no de escarmentado —que no soy tan cuerdo—, sino de cansado. Como obstinado pecador, determiné, consultándolo primero con la Grajal, de pasarme a Indias con ella, a ver si, mudando mundo y tierra, mejoría mi suerte. Y fueme peor, como v.m. verá en la segunda parte, pues nunca mejora su estado quien muda solamente de lugar, y no de vida y costumbres. (p. 280)

This ending seems written in direct challenge and in response to Alemán's vision of the *pícaro*. Pablos is destined to an existence of continuing and worsening frustration. He is victimized and kept in his place.

---

13 EDMOND CROS: *L'Aristocrate...,* pp. 17-25.

In comparison with Lazarillo, Pablos' ambitions were loftier and more threatening to the social order. His goal was not only to «arrimarse a los buenos». Lazarillo was content to live off the «well-to-do», whereas Pablos wanted to be one of them. As Pablos mentions when he leaves his parents to join Don Diego Coronel in boarding school, he intends to become a gentleman. The negative corollary of this desire to move up in society is to turn his back on his family («negar la sangre», p. 148), because of whom he feels intense shame. At first Pablos hopes to be virtuous, but after his dreadful experiences at the university, he adopts the picaresque ethic of survival. He heeds the old adage, «haz como vieres»; he behaves like those around him and becomes a «bellaco», resorting to stealth, guile, and deception to make his way in the world. His final effort at entry into the *hidalgo class* by marrying Doña Ana, a cousin of his old friend and master, Don Diego Coronel, is resolutely defeated when he is beaten by Don Diego's henchmen. «Así paran los pícaros mal nacidos» (p. 241), is their parting sally. Pablos' unseemly ambitions are the motivating force behind his actions throughout the work. These ambitions far exceed his station in life. Pablos is trapped from the beginning by his ignominious birth at the bottom of a society that Quevedo frequently satirized both in *El Buscón* and in other works as well. This society is satirized in *El Buscón* from Pablos' point of view, as he looks back over his life from its earliest days until he embarked for America.

Parody, Satire, and the Reader

Pablo's pretensions are greater than any other *pícaro*'s and he is punished more dramatically. The exaggerated and grotesque quality of the narration has given rise to speculations that the work is a parody of the picaresque.[14] Everything in the *Buscón* is more extreme than ever before, so much so that the conventions of mimetic fiction are often abandoned. Pablos' shame and ambition are far greater, his parents and other relatives more reprehensible, the tricks more vile, the excrement and spittle more plentiful, and appearances more deceitful in *El Buscón* than in other picaresque works. The trajectory of Pablos' adventures in which his end is worse than his beginning («y fueme peor», p. 280) is unwavering. The character of the *pícaro*, the hyperbolic treatment given to certain elements of the text, and the sense bestowed on the whole of the work by its ending induce the reader to interpret the *Buscón* as a literary parody of the picaresque, an intertextual creation that rejects and transgresses the past texts on which it is modeled. One dimension of *El Buscón*, therefore, is that it contains implicitly a critical or negative reading of previous

---

[14] SEGUNDO SERRANO PONCELA: «*El Buscón*, ¿parodia picaresca?», in *Del Romancero a Machado* (Caracas: Ediciones de la Biblioteca. Universidad Central de Venezuela, 1962), pp. 87-103; HARRY SIEBER: «Apostrophes en *El Buscón*: An Approach to Quevedo's Narrative Technique», *MLN*, 83 (1968), 178-211; and M. and C. CAVILLAC: «A propos de *Buscón* et de *Guzmán*», *Bulletin Hispanique*, 75 (1973), 114-131.

picaresque novels. It is an «imitation with a vengeance»,[15] magnifying the faults of former *pícaros,* disparaging the form of their tales, and casting doubt on the validity of their conclusions. A parodic reading of *El Buscón* introduces a cleft between the author-in-the-text and the fictitious narrator, and prompts the reader to react to Pablos on a number of different levels. The parodic dimension of the work accounts for the conflict readers have felt between author and narrator. Pablos is the parody of a *pícaro* and, as narrator, the justifiably angry voice that satirizes the world he encounters by viewing it through a flawed lens.[16]

Quevedo was, in fact, the foremost satirist of his age. His chief weapons are *ingenio, agudeza,* puns, grotesque imagery, conceits, and euphemisms, all devoted to abuse at its wittiest. It is perhaps strange, therefore, that interpretations of *El Buscón* have tended to polarize around the two extreme interpretations of the novel mentioned earlier: one that it is a *serious* psychological study of a delinquent and the other that it is a *comic* book of jokes.[17] No one need doubt the fundamentally serious purpose of satirical works, however frivolous the means to that end.

Language, Humor, and Style

Two aspects of *El Buscón,* one structural and the other linguistic, imbue the work with a disjunctive or non-cohesive quality. One is its parodic structure and the other its polysemic language which entails frequent offshoots from the text. Since the *pícaro* is parodied and in the end suppressed, one senses a conflict between the author's and the *pícaro's* voice. Many have assumed that the humor of the work is part of the attack by the author on the protagonist.[18] However, the humorist is the mature Pablos himself, looking back over his life. The black humour may be interpreted, I think, as a defense mechanism against a world which has treated him cruelly.

[15] ULRICH WEISSTEIN: «Parody, Travesty, and Burlesque: Imitations with a Vengeance», in *Actes du IV Congres de L'Association International de Littérature Comparée* (The Hague and Paris: Mouton, 1966), pp. 803-811.

[16] TUVIA SHLONSKY: «Literary Parody; Remarks on its Method and Function», in *Proceedings of the AILC/ICLA,* IV, vol. 2, pp. 797-801, defines parody as an imitation of another literary work or some of its elements that «attempts to disrealize the norms that the original tries to realize». According to Shlonsky, pure parody maintains a relationship with literature alone. Hence, my distinction between satire, which is aimed at society or the actual inhabitants of the world, and parody, whose object is literary. Parody and satire are not only determining semantic structures of *El Buscón* but also of other of Quevedo's works. Some of his sonnets, such as «La Nariz» and the mock heroic poem «Poema heroico de las necedades y locuras de Orlando el enamorado» are literary parodies. *Los Sueños y La Hora de Todos* are ironic and satirical dream visions in which social criticism and an underlying attitude of *desengaño* are easily detected. *El Buscón* is perhaps unique among his works in that the vehicle of the satire is also a literary parody.

[17] ALEXANDER PARKER in *Los Pícaros en la Literatura* (1967; Madrid: Gredos, 1971), p. 108, states: «Escribe un libro sarcástico y gracioso de verdad, pero donde la psicología de la delincuencia está concebida muy en serio y donde el ingenio sigue unas pautas estructurales que se ajustan a la descripción interior del protagonista.»

[18] See FRANCISCO RICO: *La Picaresca y el punto de vista,* pp. 127, 128; and EDWIN WILLIAMSON: «Conflict...», p. 47.

Quevedo does not allow Pablos to succeed in this world, and he thus becomes the spokesman and agent for a satirical vision while remaining helpless, ineffectual, and parodied, but not silenced. He is consigned to limbo, as certainly as Gulliver is on the Lilliputians' wagon.

Given the narrator's level of frustration, his decisions, observations, and style are not surprising. His humor effectively shatters reality as an angry boy roils the surface of a pond by throwing stones. The disturbed surface returns to normal after leaving the observer with a distorted reflection of the world. In the same way, the reader may consider the distortions in the text in relation to what is familiar to him and reexamine mimetic reality and social values.

The difficulty is that the continuity of the narrative is often interrupted by the dense and ambiguous quality of its language. This happens frequently in descriptions which lose their reality in that one is not certain whether they are representational or are merely included for the sake of punning. One feels that linguistic playfulness is more responsible for the course of the narrative than the conventions of realistic fiction: verisimilitude in the characterization, motivation, dialogue, and action of the fictional characters. A case in point is Pablos' description of his father, which includes the following pun: «Dicen que era de muy buena cepa; y según él bebió, puédese muy bien creer» (p. 15). Pablos literally cannot resist the temptation to depart from the text whenever a word play suggests itself, or, alternatively, selects material with that propensity in mind. Yet the pleasure of the text resides in its disruptive and polysemic nature, and the narrative style accomplishes the dual aesthetic purpose suggested in the prologue — to tell jokes as well as the story of a *pícaro*'s life to the reader. The style is expressive of a vision that is a result of the character and experience of the *pícaro*. What Pablos could not change, he can laugh at in retrospect. The composition of Pablos' satirical portrait of contemporary society, seen from the ever-changing perspective provided by his picaresque journey, is as important a feature of the work as is the effect of those travels on Pablos as an individual.

It remains to examine other principal features of *El Buscón*'s style, and further describe the effect of the narration on the reader in regard to its language. The way in which black humor, euphemisms, and conceits construct a defensive rampart against a darker world is evident from the beginning pages, when Pablos' father semantically elevates his ignominious office of *barbero* by calling himself «tundidor de mejillas y sastre de barbas». He belies his humble station in life with pretentious artifice, deluding himself and others with words. Pablos inherits his father's love of euphemism and linguistic play, of masking the truth with illusions, and of displacing reality with enigmatic and fanciful metaphors. The text mystifies, but also reveals. The means of mystification is the text's complicated foliage of conceits and puns, leafy tendrils from the trunk of the text which obscure its shape as they hide the dreadful real world from sight.

Language in *El Buscón* obfuscates on one level, ultimately clarifies on another. This demystifying movement or unmasking is one of the primary structural principles of the text. The effect on the reader is that of initial puzzlement, then enlightenment, shock, and laughter. Reality is nearly always a disappointment, but the pleasure of the text resides in the cleverness of the conceits and the reader's recognition of them, as well as the visual delight of the grotesque images projected.

For the images in the work are unusually graphic and almost demand visualization. Pablos continually calls attention to the pictorial quality of the text by prefacing descriptions with statements such as «era de ver» or «mire usted».[19] Once he compares a scene to a painting by Bosch (p. 171). Yet even without these interpretive instructions, the painterly quality of Quevedo's grotesque world must be apprehended by any reader. Paradoxically, the images utilized render a fragmented and distorted reality, surfaces divested of their underlying meaning and unconnected series of tableaux. Mimetic reality dissolves into components that acquire a life of their own, a phenomenon that more than one critic has labeled «cosificación».[20] But the way in which animate beings are reified is only one aspect of the surrealistic vision of Quevedo. Conversely, inanimate objects are enlivened and operate according to laws which are prescribed neither by nature nor by the conventions of mimetic representation. Reality is twisted into bizarre new shapes. Occasionally, as in the composite portrait of Cabra, a personification or archetypal portrayal may be abstracted from the accumulation of grotesque parts, each of which contribute in an additive way to highlight various manifestations of an abstract quality — in this case a stinginess resulting in his own and other's starvation. Pablos often combines several lies or hyperbolic statements to communicate a fundamental truth.

Homologous Structures and the Reader

The pattern of sentients or natural rhythm of the text, echoed in the forms of feeling evoked in the reader, is reflected in its ideology, the structure of the episodes of the narration, and language. On the level of ideology, illusions, hopes, and ideals are effectively devalued. As Cros points out:

> Remarquons en effet que le chevauchement de deux textes se fait chaque fois autour d'une expression lexicalisée («andar siempre por las iglesias», et «ser de buena cepa») qui, à un premier niveau de décodage, connote des valeurs sociales telles que le piété et la noblesse, tandis que prise dans le réseau sémantique allusif du second texte, elle éclate et se délexicalise. Ce que Francisco Rico regrette en fait c'est que cette délexicalization qu'un lecteur attentif du Buscón est tout prêt à faire lui soit imposée par la coordonnée qui suit («y no de puro cristiano» et «y según él bebía, es cosa para creer»). Mais en réalité l'expression lexicalisée est elle-même conçue comme élément d'un discours mystificateur dont la dénonciation doit être explicite.[21]

---

[19] EDMOND CROS: L'Aristocrate..., p. 84.
[20] CLAMURRO: «The Destabilized Sign...», pp. 297-301; J. CORRALES EGEA: «La novela picaresca», Insula, 24 (1969), 15; and MAURICE MOLHO: «Introduction to Romans picaresques espagnols» (Paris: Galimard, 1968), p. lxxxvii.
[21] EDMOND CROS: L'Aristocrate..., p. 66.

The experience of the *pícaro* and some other characters in the fiction also reflects the same dramatic structure of demystification and destruction. Appearances deceive only for a time. Pablos struts and postures until his deceitfulness is exposed and he is punished. Examples are the «rey de gallos» episode, his entry to the University of Alcalá, his ride on a «borrowed» horse, and his attempted wooing of Doña Ana. Pablos' ambitions, showy displays, and strutting ultimately result in his humiliation, being mired in excrement or spat upon, in his falling off his horse or being trounced. In Pablos' world the characters are given to maintaining appearances and displaying their finery — thus, his father's triumphal journey to the gallows and Don Toribio's fanciful dress. When Pablos' father is hung and when we see beneath Don Toribio's cloak, the illusory nature of this world becomes apparent. Truth and reality reassert themselves, and the reader is disillusioned or «desengañado».

The Sisyphus rhythm operates in *El Buscón* on the linguistic level as well as the narrative and ideological levels. The pattern of the experience of the *pícaro* is repeated in miniature in its prose. Reality is destabilized and disorted, and disintegrates into an aggregate of component parts, as in Cabra's portrait or the description of the clothing of the *colegio buscón*. Through the refractions of conceits and witticisms, the focus in deflected from the psychological and toward the external. An emphasis on objects and surface obscures the individuality and pain of the person undergoing the experience.[22] The predominance of physical detail has a dehumanizing effect; the sensual world becomes grotesque and almost hallucinatory, and the lack of reality of the depictions induces the reader to speculate metaphysically about what is real. Language is used as a tool of the *pícaro*'s deceits, yet finally enlightens or undeceives. Mysterious metaphors are followed by bold statements such as «Al fin, él era archipobre y protomiseria» (p. 34). Language conceals and then reveals: «... era conqueridora de voluntades y corchete de gustos que es lo mismo que alcagüeta» (p. 29). Visions of splendor are reduced to harsh reality: «salió de la cárcel con tanta honra que le acompañaron docientos cardenales sino que a ninguno llamaban 'señoría'» (p. 17). Whimsical linguistic playfulness is often followed by a rude awakening on the narrative level, as in this episode:

> Unos decían: —«¡Garbanzos negros! Sin duda son de Etiopia.» Otros decían: —«¡Garbanzos con luto! ¿Quién se les habrá muerto?» Mi amo fue el primero que se encajó una cuenta, y al mascarla se quebró un diente. (p. 45)

Thus, through the figuration of the prose, the construction of the episodes of the narration, and the devaluing of societal ideals, the reader shares in the *pícaro*'s experience of the world — disillusion and disappointment. The shape of the narration as a whole, with its emphasis on the downward spiral of the *pícaro*'s luck («fueme peor»), mirrors the same destructive or demystifying movement. Whatever is constructed in *El Buscón* finally inspires a negative response that is also embodied in some way in the text.

[22] WILLIAM H. CLAMURRO: «The Destabilized Sign...», p. 303.

In manifold ways creation is followed by destruction. Thus the life of a *pícaro* becomes as well a book of jests, for the butt of the jokes is so often Pablos himself — as much the author's scapegoat as is society. Likewise, the role of the reader as a morally, socially, and artistically superior individual is first established and then disparaged or cast aside. The status of the reader is effectively devalued by the suggestion that he may either be a *pícaro* or may be stupid enough to be deceived by a *pícaro*. (The reader's possible picaresque character can also be inferred in Roberto Duport's prologue.) Everything ends on the downbeat in *El Buscón;* and thus the rythm or figuration of the work, which operates both on the contiguous or syntagmatic and the associative or paradigmatic linguistic axes, unifies the text. *El Buscón* is a work thoroughly permeated by pessimism, and the aforementioned homologous structures readily communicate to the reader a dreadful, all-pervasive dissatisfaction with the world. The same significance attaches to the plot as well as to its rhetoric.

Nonetheless, the work evokes in the reader a number of contradictory reactions in regard to Pablos that resemble the feelings experienced in reading *Lazarillo*. As Edwin Williamson states:

> The character of Pablos remains problematical to the end: his conduct is damnable and yet the reader cannot condemn him with unembarrassed equanimity. Similarly the reader's satirical laughter is strangely unsettling: is he laughing at Pablos himself or is he laughing with Pablos at the other characters? The butt of the satire remains unclear and elusive. Reading *El Buscón* is an exercise in which one is put through different hoops of sympathy, disgust, amusement and moral disapproval, without leaping clear to a position of assured judgment.[23]

The attitude displayed by the implied author toward his fictional narrator and the network of negative responses and destructive treatment given to the characters, language, objects, and ideology of *El Buscón* all induce a range of contradictory responses. There are no redeeming features in the fictional world of *El Buscón* to inspire the reader's loyalty. As. H. L. Mencken once said, satire is diagnostic, rather than therapeutic [24] — the recognition of thorny, unresolved problems. One of the usual pleasures of satire for the reader is the flash of recognition from a safe distance. Quevedo at first creates a role for the reader in which he is allowed to enjoy that stance, but later removes the reader from his pedestal by offering him new vantage points from which to contemplate himself in the context of the picaresque world.

Like *Lazarillo, El Buscón* is an example of a work that transforms carnivalesque structures into literary form. Pablos is very much like that masked carnivalesque scapegoat figure —actualized in the «rey de gallos» episode— that, after the brief celebration of his ritual dance, returns to his original unmasked lowly state. *El Buscón* is a fundamentally conser-

---

[23] EDWIN WILLIAMSON: «Conflict...», p. 46.
[24] LEONARD FEINBERG in *Introduction to Satire* (Ames, Iowa: Iowa State University Press, 1967), p. 10, quotes the following: «'My business', said Mencken, 'is diagnosis, not therapeutics'.»

vative work, an escape-valve to defuse anger and aggression, an *exposé* of the follies of an age that is in no way suggestive of change. As in *Lazarillo,* some of the contradictions experienced by readers of the work may derive from regarding the humor as hostile to Pablos and the «I» as the enemy «other», rather than as one of us and a representative of mankind. Carnival is properly cathartic only if it is a participatory experience. Other contradictions in attitude or response on the part of the reader may be due to the parodic dimension of the text (which has the effect of making Pablos the «butt of the satire», as Williamson suggests) and the resulting rift between author and narrator.

For Quevedo treats his *pícaro* harshly, and given the carnivalesque duality of destruction and regeneration, destruction plays the more important role in *El Buscón.* It is as though the rise of the *pícaro* in literature and in life threatened the stability and hierarchical order of things. Quevedo hated that order in some ways, yet could not envision any palatable changes. His vision is one of a fragmented society in the process of breaking up, yet he resists the success of the *pícaro* as not at all permissible. Rather, the *pícaro* is interpreted as another sign of disintegration, and no political change is advocated as a cure for social ills. Yet carnivalistic structures are strained in *El Buscón,* as though carnivals were no longer conservative, cathartic rituals designed to maintain the *status quo,* but rather were thought to be inflammatory and, perhaps ultimately, revolutionary. As omnipotent author, Quevedo punishes society with satire and his upstart *pícaro* with defeat. For Quevedo and for Pablos, therefore, the pen must be mightier than the sword. It is through the voice and eyes of Pablos that Quevedo projects a palpable vision of moral and political corruption with no solution in sight.

CHAPTER V

CONCLUSIONS AND POSSIBILITIES
FOR FURTHER STUDY

In this study I have utilized an intertextual approach to explore the nature of the relationships prescribed between the three principal works of the picaresque genre and their readers past and present, as well as the links between the works themselves. The semantic structures of each novel depend on the attitudes of the reader toward the narrator and toward society as represented in the fiction. Important considerations in this regard have been the role a fictitious reader or the presence of one or more hypothetical readers as structures whereby the real reader is invited to fictionalize himself in regard to the text. The analysis of each work has been contingent upon regarding reading as a dynamic process, both sequential and intertextual. In this way I have been able to account for individual and historical differences in interpretations of the texts. In a sense, my study has been an attempt to approximate a meta-reading of the texts by examining the contexts of various previous interpretations and thus their predispositions and limitations.

In each novel the use of a fictitious or hypothetical reader structures the narration so that the reader experiences it in the appropriate way. In Chapter II, I described how Lazarillo, the fictitious narrator, directs his narration to the real reader through a kaleidoscope of *destinataires*, the most important of whom is the fictional reader, Vuestra Merced. The tone and the tenor of Lazarillo's tale vary according to the *destinataire* he addresses. The author of *Lazarillo*, by thus subtly varying the perspective from which the reader views his protagonist, alternatively presents Lazarillo as an amusing friend and kindred spirit and as a reprehensible adult, a cuckold who is implicated in the world satirized. The last *tratado* in particular induces the reader to take an ironic view of Lazarillo by explaining the *caso* mentioned in the prologue. The reader is challenged by the shocking nature of the conclusion to reassess the work as a whole and to relate Lazarillo the child to Lázaro the adult.

Other factors contribute to the reader's oscillation in regarding *Lazarillo* as now a comic now an ironic work. The carnivalesque participatory humor, Lazarillo's humanity and gaiety, and the emphasis on the material facts of existence cause the reader to sympathize with Lazarillo and share his experience. The works's acerbic wit, its parodic elements, some of its innovations in regard to the literature of the past, the social satire, and Lazarillo's final compromise elicit an ironic reading of the work. The dual comic and ironic structure and the differing response of Renaissance and contemporary readers to comedy are the characteristics of the work most responsible for the variety of responses the work has evoked, possibilities also prefigured in the fictitious responses of the *destinataires,* who function as prisms through which the work is filtered. The tale emanates from a single source, but is refracted through its *destinataires* to the reader.

Guzmán·   *Guzmán de Alfarache,* for all its echoes and amplifications of *Lazarillo,* is a work imbued with an entirely different structure and spirit. Its development might be described as dialogical, because the presence of a hypothetical reader antagonistic to Guzmán so intensely dominates the text. This hypothetical reader is placed in an accusatory or hostile position vis-à-vis the narrator, who correspondingly assumes a defensive posture. In the prologue, the potential readership is polarized, and a dichotomy is posited between the ideal discreet reader, a kindly and protective patron who is interested in his own moral betterment, and the vicious, ignorant, and tasteless *vulgo.* In the text the hypothetical reader criticizes Guzmán, who defends, explains, and exonerates himself, fearful lest the reader delight only in the picaresque adventures of the work, ignoring its moral doctrine and taking offense at its long-winded and digressive style. The imagery of the work confirms the paranoid mistrust that the disillusioned, humiliated, and frustrated narrator feels in regard to the world and the reader.

The work is structured in an oxymoronic configuration, the *conseja* providing the numerous bad examples which inspire the *consejo.* The contradictions between narrative and doctrine and the resulting lack of organic unity, perhaps disconcerting to modern readers, were probably not particularly bothersome to the seventeenth-century audience. Such was accustomed to reading loosely connected compendia of moral teachings in which the narrative was of secondary importance. Doctrine and narrative should be related as indicated in the prologue, which states that the work purports to «enseñar por su contrario la forma de bien vivir» (I, p. 43).

An intertextual approach has been particularly apt in deciphering the parodic structures of *El Buscón* and its network of negativities elaborated in response to past picaresque novels, contemporary society, mimetic reality, and even to the reader himself. The prologue indicates the dual character of the work, being both the *tour de force* of a stylist and the autobiography of a *pícaro.* Quevedo parodies both the *pícaro* and the picaresque, and even the *pícaro*'s narrative convention of frequently addressing the reader. Pablos directs himself to the reader at his most outlandish moments, as if to call attention to his own ridiculous posturing and grotesque vision of the world. In contrast to *Lazarillo* and *Guzmán, El Buscón* establishes a role for the reader only to dissipate it by abruptly introducing several alternative roles and therefore readings. All these readings are for the most part hostile to Pablos and his social pretensions.

One of the most important consequences of the technique of addressing a fictional reader in *Lazarillo, Guzmán,* and *El Buscón* is to indicate to the real reader that *pícaros* are unreliable narrators. Lázaro appears to be telling his life to a judge or an authority figure of superior social status, and one may suspect that he is attempting to present himself in as favorable a light as possible. The critical and hostile reaction that the hypothetical reader often displays in regard to Guzmán's narration establishes a similar suspicious distance between the narrator and the real reader. Pablos, in addressing the reader at the most outrageous moments of his narration, reveals similar doubts about the reception of his version of his life. The reader is led to suspect that the *pícaro*'s tale is the confession of a liar. The frequent direct addresses to the fictional reader call the real reader's attention to the narrator himself in the process of narrating, and away from the events narrated. They deliberately interrupt the persuasive flow of the narration, a reminder of the *pícaro*'s cunning in the telling of his tale.

The picaresque consists of the *pícaro*'s recollection of his past life. He is a writer who is implicitly presenting himself as an amusing and astute critic of society to those of superior social status or in authority over him. Though the views of the *pícaro* are cynical and even subversive, he is allowed to entertain and ridicule, but not to destroy or change the social order. Nor does the *pícaro* transcend his position at the bottom rung of the social ladder. The endings of each novel corroborate these conclusions. Lazarillo has achieved a modest security yet sacrificed his honor, and his satisfaction is viewed with apparent irony by the author. Guzmán is serving a term in the galley ships. Quevedo clearly expects no change for the better in Pablos' character or social situation, and *El Buscón* terminates with a pessimistic assessment of his future. «Y fueme peor, como vuesa merced verá en la segunda parte, pues nunca mejora su estado quien muda solamente de lugar, y no de vida y costumbres.» The *pícaro* is destined by his low birth to remain that way, because his status at birth determines his status for life. The *pícaro* repeats the mistakes of his elders, escaping neither his environment nor the «fuerza de la sangre». The *pícaro* can do no more than speak his piece, and to a public that is by no means whole-heartedly or consistently sympathetic. He cannot alter the *status quo*. Thus, as a recent article points out, «a psychodrama is staged in the text in which authority is subverted and preserved at the same time».[1]

Cervantes, who wrote several works that play with the conventions of the picaresque genre or contain readings of or reactions to picaresque novels, indicates that he likewise regards the *pícaro* as an unreliable narrator. In the *Coloquio de los Perros* his *pícaro*-narrators are dogs, dream-vision figures conjured up by a soldier-*pícaro* Campuzano, who is recovering from syphilis. Ginés de Pasamonte in the *Quijote* is the greatest «bellaco» of the *galeotes,* all tricksters who indulge in word-plays so that Don Quijote misinterprets the reasons for their incarceration. Thus it can be surmised that this greatest of seventeenth-century readers considered the *pícaro* an untrustworthy narrator. In other works, such as the *Ilustre Fregona* and *Rinconete y Cortadillo*, Cervantes' *pícaro*-protagonists are happier and less

---

[1] ROBERTO GONZÁLEZ ECHEVARRÍA: «The Life and Adventures of Cipión: Cervantes and the Picaresque», *Diacritics* (Sept. 1980), pp. 18-22.

frustrated than other *pícaros*. They freely set off in search of picaresque adventures and just as easily abandon this life style when they wish. Cervantes regards the *pícaro* as a player on life's stage and addresses the philosophical implications of his *modus vivendi* more than its socio-political consequences. The hypothetical reader is given his autonomy, left free to be entertained, and is not placed in the position of authority or judge vis-à-vis the *pícaro*. Cervantes, it appears, rejected the type of relationship established between narrator and reader implicit in other picaresque novels, as well as their autobiographical form and philosophy of life.

Even in the works under discussion —*Lazarillo, Guzmán,* and *El Buscón*— the authoritative, superior, or critical stance accorded to the reader is not consistently sustained. The reader may variously laugh *at* and then *with* the *pícaro*, delighted by the *pícaro*'s antics and jokes. Or, amusement may turn to sympathy of a more serious sort as the reader is drawn into the *pícaro*'s precarious experience — an ever-present option. Each author establishes strategies whereby the reader's response to the *pícaro*-protagonist will vary and he will alternatively see himself as better than, no better than, or even inferior to the *pícaro*. The narrations mirror the reader's own propensity for folly and periodically remind him of this. The ambiguity evoked in the reader's response is reinforced by the periodic discord between the narrator's voice and the author's. In all these works the author-in-the-text maintains some ironic distance from his linguistically playful protagonist and overtly expresses disapproval of, for example, Lazarillo's marriage, Guzmán's garrulousness and vindictive nature, and Pablos' unseemly ambition as a *parvenu*. On the three, Pablos is the most cruelly treated, and becomes a parody of his predecessors.

The author's attitude toward his protagonist somewhat relativizes the dogmatic or unitary point of view often proposed as essential to the poetics of the picaresque novel. In any case, this monolithic perspective on the world is revealed and concealed according to the *pícaro*-protagonist's obvious artfulness. His confession and self-dramatization are affected by his public's anticipated response. We are presented with a series of acts featuring the *pícaro* in various roles and a variety of disguises. The use of the image of a hypothetical reader becomes, in effect, a way of promoting a certain reading to which, however, there are alternatives. The narrator's singular perspective is balanced by the shifting perspective granted the reader through the agency of several responsive *destinataires*. Lazarillo is sometimes aware of the presence of Vuestra Merced, and at other times addresses God or himself in *apartes*, records the reactions of various spectators to his experiences, and so on. Guzmán alternatively considers the response of an ideal reader, the *vulgo*, the critical and hostile reader whom he takes for granted, the reader who loves fable and ignores doctrine, and the imperfect reader who needs to be taught. *El Buscón* also considers the different sort of readers whom the work might attract, after an initial deference to a reader who is shocked by Pablos' grotesque wit, and yet, somewhat paradoxically, eager to be amused. All the works establish a certain tension between narrator and hypothetical reader, distanced by social status, mistrust, or differences in attitude and taste. At the same time, all reflect an attempt to appeal to various types of readers and contain the structures or schema to make more than one reading possible. Thus the real reader is inclined to actively pursue an interpretation that will be dependent not only on the strategies set forth in the text, but also on his own attitudes toward society and the individual.

In this regard, the picaresque novel has been able to exercise a wide appeal to readers of various political persuasions through the centuries. However, it can be surmised that modern readings differ significantly from those of contemporary times in that the modern reader's understanding of the picaresque novels is affected by his familiarity with the modern novel and protest literature. Many readers, some with anti-social inclinations themselves, are accustomed to view the familiar literary character of rebel or anti-hero sympathetically and assume the same attitudes to have been prevalent among sixteenth and seventeenth-century authors and readers. The result has been a somewhat distorted vision of the picaresque in that the author's point of view has been too closely associated with the *pícaro*'s; nor has the importance of the use of rhetoric as persuasion been sufficiently recognized as manipulator or modulator of the reader's response. Furthermore, the aims of modern interpretation, whether reader oriented or not, pertain to the discovery of the work's significance, whereas Renaissance and Baroque literature was designed to achieve certain effects in the reader and to influence his behavior. The way in which the reader was expected to become involved in the text was therefore different, requiring his active participation not to decipher meaning, but to experience directly the action and to be affected emotionally by the power and force of the language.[2] Oddly enough, the contemporary critical focus on reading as an activity brings the modern reader closer to the participatory experience of the text assumed in past times. The recent interest in the carnivalesque structures inherent to Renaissance and post-Renaissance literature has clarified the nature of expected reader response of the time and the spirit of this incipient protest literature.

To seek the seeds of modernity in the problematic and unresolved quality of the picaresque should not be construed as a misreading. The dynamic at work between Spain's peculiar social and political structure and the emergence of the picaresque novel is not altogether clear. The literature of the Renaissance has been called a «literature of patronage», and was in part designed to achieve certain effects in socio-political terms. The representation of reality often served to exert a moral influence on the individual to the direct benefit of the state and the aristocracy in power.[3] Spain's unusual social structure and the dearth of studies on

---

[2] JANE P. TOMKINS: «The Reader in History», in *Reader-Response Criticism,* ed. Jane P. Tomkins (Baltimore and London: Johns Hopkins University Press, 1980), pp. 201-206.

[3] JANE P. TOMKINS: «The Reader in History», pp. 207, 208, wherein she cites BERNARD WEINBERG: *History of Literary Criticism in the Italian Renaissance* (Chicago: The University of Chicago Press, 1961) and ARTHUR MAROTTI: «John Donne and the Rewards of Patronage», *Patronage in the Renaissance,* eds. Stephen Orgel and Guy Lyttle (Princeton: Princeton University Press, 1981).

literary and artistic patrons of the Golden Age leave many unanswered questions about the relationship of this non-heroic mimesis to the reading public to which it was addressed. As I have previously indicated, a socio-historical study of the patrons of the picaresque might further illuminate the genesis of this fascinating and strident genre.[4] The internal analysis of the works undertaken in this study suggests that the authors of *Lazarillo* and *Guzmán* deliberately catered to a highly varied reading public and structured their works accordingly. Because of their ambiguity, conflictive nature, and susceptibility to a variety of readings, *Guzmán* and *Lazarillo* seem atypical of the literature of patronage. *El Buscón* better conforms to the suggested paradigm, since Quevedo maintains the *status quo* by ridiculing the *pícaro*'s social pretensions while excluding the aristocracy in his bitter satire of many facets of society. The analysis of other picaresque works might further answer some of the still unresolved questions about picaresque narrative and the reading public for whom it was first destined.

[4] See Chapter I, note 15.

BIBLIOGRAPHY

ABAD, FRANCISCO: «Ideario político y mentalidad señorial de Quevedo», *CHA*, 361-362 (1980), 85-92.

ABRAMS, FRED: «To Whom Was the Anonymous *Lazarillo de Tormes* Dedicated?», *Romance Notes*, 8 (1966), 273-277.

AGUERA, VICTORIO G.: «La salvación del cristiano nuevo en *Guzmán de Alfarache*», *Hispania*, 57 (1974), 23-30.

— «Nueva interpretación del episodio 'Rey de gallos' del *Buscón*», *Hispanófila*, 49 (1973), 33-40.

— «Notas sobre las burlas de Alcalá de *La Vida del Buscón*», *Romance Notes*, 13 (1972), 503-506.

ALEMÁN, MATEO: *Guzmán de Alfarache*, ed. Samuel Gili Gaya. Madrid: Espasa-Calpe, 1972.

ALONSO, DÁMASO: «El realismo psicológico en el *Lazarillo*», in *De los Siglos oscuros al de Oro*, Madrid: Editorial Gredos, 1958.

ARIAS, JOAN: *Guzmán de Alfarache: the Urepentant Narrator*, London: Tamesis, 1977.

— «Metaphor and Meaning: Reflections on a Central Episode of the *Guzmán de Alfarache*», *Mester*, X (1981), 14-20.

AZAR, INÉS: «Meaning, Intention, and the Written Text: Anthony Close's Approach to Don Quijote and its Critics», *MLN*, 96, no. 2 (March 1981), p. 444.

BAGBY, A. I.: «The Conventional Golden Age *Pícaro* and Quevedo's Criminal *Pícaro*», *KRQ*, 14 (1967), 311-319.

BAKHTIN, MIKHAIL: *The Dialogic Imagination*, trans. Caryl Emerson and Michael Holquist, Austin and London: Univ. of Texas Press, 1981.

— *Problems of Dostoevsky's Poetics*, trans. R. W. Rotsel, USA: Ardis, 1973.

— *Rabelais and His World*, trans. Helen Iswolsky, Cambridge, Mass., and London: The M.I.T. Press, 1965.

BALAKIAN, ANNA: «Influence and Literary Fortune; the Equivocal Junction of Two Methods», *YGCL*, No. 11 (1962), 24-31.

BARNOUW, DAGMAR: «Critics in the Act of Reading», *Poetics Today*, 1:4 (1980), 213-222.

BARTHES, ROLAND: *Elements of Semiology*, trans. Annette Lavers and Colin Smith, New York: Hill and Wang, 1967.

— *The Pleasure of the Text*, trans. Richard Miller, New York: Hill and Wang, 1975.

BASDEKIS, DEMETRIOS: «Cervantes in Unamuno: Towards a Clarification», *RR*, 60, No. 3 (October 1969), 178-185.

BATAILLON, MARCEL: *Novedad y fecundidad del Lazarillo de Tormes*, Madrid: Ediciones Anaya, 1968.

— *Pícaros y Picaresca*, Madrid: Taurus, 1969.

BELL, A.: «The Rhetoric of Self Defense of Lázaro de Tormes», *MLR*, 68 (1973), 84-93.

113

BJORNSON, RICHARD: «Moral Blindness in Quevedo's *El Buscón*», *RR*, 67 (1976), 50-59.
— *The Picaresque Hero in European Fiction*, Madison: The Univ. of Wisconsin Press, 1977.
BLACKBURN, ALEXANDER: *The Myth of the Pícaro*, Chapel Hill: The Univ. of North Carolina Press, 1979.
BLANCO AGUINAGA, CARLOS: «Cervantes y la picaresca. Notas sobre dos tipos de realismo», *NRFH*, 11 (1957), 313-342.
BLEIBERG, GERMÁN: «Mateo Alemán y los galeotes», *Revista de Occidente*, 39 (1966), 330-363.
— «Nuevos datos biográficos de Mateo Alemán», *Actas del Segundo Congreso Internacional de Nijmegen*, 1967, 25-50.
BLOOM, HAROLD: *The Anxiety of Influence. A Theory of Poetry*, New York: Oxford University Press, 1973.
— *A Map of Misreading*, New York: Oxford University Press, 1975.
BOOTH, WAYNE C.: *The Rhetoric of Fiction*, Chicago and London: The Univ. of Chicago Press, 1961.
BRANCAFORTE, BENITO: *Guzmán de Alfarache: ¿Conversión o proceso de degradación?*, Madison: Hispanic Seminary of Medieval Studies, 1980.
BRAUDEL, FERNAND: *The Mediterranean and the Mediterranean World in the Age of Philip II*, vol. II, trans. Siân Reynolds, London: Collins, 1972.
BRINKER, MENACHEM: «Two Phenomenologies of Reading: Ingarden and Iser on Textual Indeterminacy», *Poetics Today*, 1:4 (1980), 203-212.
BROWN, NORMAN O.: *Life Against Death*, New York: Vintage Books, 1959.
BURKE, KENNETH: «Four Master Tropes», in *A Grammar of Motives*. 1945; rpt. Berkeley and Los Angeles: Univ. of California Press, 1969.
CAREY, DOUGLAS M.: «Asides and Interiority in *Lazarillo de Tormes*», *Studies in Philology*, 66 (1969), 119-134.
— «Lazarillo de Tormes and the Quest for Authority», *PMLA*, 94 (1979), 36-46.
CARO BAROJA, JULIO: *El Carnaval (Análisis Histórico-Cultural)*, 2nd. ed., Madrid: Taurus, 1979.
CASTRO, AMÉRICO: «Perspectiva de la Novela Picaresca», in *Hacia Cervantes*, Madrid: Taurus, 1967.
CAVILLAC, M. and C.: «A propos de *Buscón* et de *Guzmán*», *BH*, 75 (1973), 114-131.
CHANDLER, FRANK W.: *Romances of Roguery*, New York: Macmillan, 1899.
CHEVALIER, MAXIME: *Lecturas y Lectores en la España de los Siglos XVI y XVII*, Madrid: Ediciones Turner, 1976.
CHORPENNING, JOSEPH F.: «Classical satire and *La vida del Buscón*», *Neophilogus*, LXI (1977), 212-219.
CLAMURRO, WILLIAM H.: «The Destabilized Sign: Word and Form in Quevedo's *Buscón*», *MLN*, 95, No. 2 (March 1980), 295-311.
CORRALES EGEA, J.: «La novela picaresca», *Insula*, 24 (1969), 3-15.
CORTÁZAR, CELINA S. DE: «Notas para el estudio de la estructura del *Guzmán de Alfarache*», *Filología*, 8 (1962), 79-95.
CRIADO DE VAL, MANUEL, ed.: *La Picaresca: Orígenes, Textos y Estructuras*, Madrid: Fundación Universitaria Española, 1979.
CROS, EDMOND: *Protée et le Gueux*, Paris: Didier, 1967.
— *L'Aristocrate et le Carnaval des Gueux*, Montpellier: Publication du Centre d'Études Sociocritique U.E.R., II, Université Paul Valéry, 1975.
— «Semántica y estructuras sociales en el *L. de T.*», *Revista Hispánica Moderna*, 39, No. 3 (1976-1977), 79-84.
CROSBY, JAMES O.: *Guía bibliográfica para el estudio crítico de Quevedo*, London: Grant & Cutler, 1976.

CRUICKSHANK, D. W.: «Literature and the booktrade in Golden Age Spain», *MLR,* LXXIII (1978), 799-824.

CULLER, JONATHAN D.: *Structuralist Poetics; Structuralism, Linguistics, and the Study of Literature,* Ithaca, Cornell Univ. Press, 1975.

CURTIUS, ERNST ROBERT: *European Literature and the Latin Middle Ages,* 1963; rpt. Princeton: Princeton Univ. Press, 1973.

DE MAN, PAUL: «Autobiography as Defacement», *MLN,* 94 (1979), 919-930.

DEMARIA, ROBERT, Jr.: «The Ideal Reader: A Critical Fiction», *PMLA,* 93 (1978), 463-474.

DE RIQUER, MARTÍN: *La Celestina y Lazarillos,* Barcelona: Vergara Editorial, 1959.

DEYERMOND, ALAN: «The Corrupted Vision: Further Thoughts on Lazarillo de Tormes», *Forum for Modern Language Studies,* I (1965), 246-249.

DÍAZ MIGOYO, GONZALO: *Estructura de la Novela. Anatomía de 'El Buscón',* Madrid: Editorial Fundamentos, 1978.

DOLEZEL, LUBOMÍR: «Eco and His Model Reader», *Poetics Today,* 1:4 (1980), 181-188.

DUCROT, OSWALD, and TODOROV, TZVETAN: *Dictionnaire Encyclopédique des Sciences du Langage.* Paris: Editions de Seuil, 1972.

DUNN, PETER N.: «El individuo y la sociedad en *La Vida del Buscón*», *BH,* 52 (1950), 375-396.

— *The Spanish Picaresque Novel,* Boston: Twayne, 1979.

— «Problems of a model for the picaresque and the case of Quevedo's *Buscón*», *BHS,* LIX (1982), 95-105.

DURÁN, MANUEL: «El Quijote a través del prisma de Mikhail Bakhtine: Carnaval, disfraces, escatología y locura», in *Cervantes and the Renaissance,* ed. M. D. McGaha, Easton, Pa.: Juan de la Cuesta, 1980.

DURAND, FRANK: «The Author and Lázaro: Levels of Comic Meaning», *BHS,* 45, no. 2 (1968), 89-101.

ECO, UMBERTO: *The Role of the Reader: Explorations in the Semiotics of Texts,* Bloomington-London: Indiana Univ. Press, 1979.

EISENBERG, DANIEL: «Who Read the Romances of Chivalry», *KRQ,* XX (1973), 209-233.

— «Does the picaresque novel exist?», *KRQ,* XXVI (1979), 201-219.

EISENSTEIN, ELIZABETH: *The Printing Press as an Agent of Change,* Cambridge: Cambridge Univ. Press, 1979.

ELLIOT, R. C.: *The Power of Satire: Magic, Ritual, Art,* Princeton: Princeton Univ. Press, 1960.

EL SAFFAR, RUTH S.: *Distance and Control in Don Quixote,* Chapel Hill: North Carolina Studies in Romance Languages and Literatures, No. 147, 1975.

— *Novel to Romance. A Study of Cervantes's Novelas ejemplares,* Baltimore: Johns Hopkins Univ. Press, 1974.

FEINBERG, LEONARD: *Introduction to Satire,* Ames, Ia.: University Press, 1967.

FETTERLEY, JUDITH: *The Resistive Reader,* Bloomington and London: Indiana Univ. Press, 1978.

FISH, STANLEY: *Self-Consuming Artifacts. The Experience of XVII Century Literature,* Berkeley, Los Angeles, and London: University of California Press, 1972.

— *Surprised by Sin. The Reader in Paradise Lost,* London, Melbourne, and Toronto: Macmillan; New York: St. Martin's Press, 1967.

FOUCAULT, MICHEL: *The Order of Things,* trans. *Les Mots et les Choses,* 1966; rpt. New York: Random House, 1973.

FRIEDMAN, NORMAN: «Point of View in Fiction: The Development of a Critical Concept», *PMLA,* 70 (1955), 1160-1184.

FRYE, NORTHRUP: *Anatomy of Criticism. Four Essays,* Princeton: Princeton Univ. Press, 1973.

GADAMER, HANS GEORG: *Wahrheit und Methode,* Tubingen: Mohr, 1960. In English, *Truth and Methode,* trans. Garret Barden and John Cumming, New York: Seabury Press, 1975.

GIBSON, WALTER: «Authors, Speakers, Readers, and Mock Readers», *College English,* 9 (February 1950), 265-269.

GILMAN, STEPHEN: «The Death of Lazarillo de Tormes», *PMLA,* 81 (1966), 149-166.

GÓMEZ-MORIANA, ANTONIO: «La subversión del discurso ritual; una lectura intertextual del *Lazarillo de Tormes*», *Imprévue* (1980-1981), 63-89.

GONZÁLEZ ECHEVERRÍA, ROBERTO: «The Life and Adventures of Cipión: Cervantes and the Picaresque», *Diacritics* (September 1980), 15-26.

GREEN, OTIS H.: «On the Attitude toward the *Vulgo* in the Spanish *Siglo de Oro*», *Studies in the Renaissance,* 4 (1957), 190-200.

GREIMAS, A. J.: *Sémantique Structurale,* Paris: Mouton, 1966.

GUILLÉN, CLAUDIO: «La disposición temporal del *Lazarillo de Tormes*», *HR,* 25 (1957), 264-279.

— *Literature as System.* Princeton: Princeton Univ. Press, 1971.

HERNADI, PAUL: *Beyond Genre.* Ithaca, N. Y.: Cornell Univ. Press, 1972.

HERRERO, JAVIER: «The Great Icons of *Lazarillo:* the Bull, the Wine, the Sausage, and the Turnip», *Ideologies and Literature,* 1, No. 5 (Jan.-Feb., 1978), 3-18.

— «The Ending of *Lazarillo:* The Wine Against the Water», *MLN,* 93 (1978), 313-319.

— «Renaissance Poverty and Lazarillo's Family: The Birth of the Picaresque Genre», *PMLA,* 94 (October 1979), 876-886.

HIGHET, GILBERT: *The Anatomy of Satire,* Princeton: Princeton Univ. Press, 1962.

IFFLAND, JAMES: «Pablos' Voice: His Master's? A Freudian Approach to Wit in *El Buscón*», *RF,* 91 (1979), 215-243.

ISER, WOLFGANG: *The Act of Reading. A Theory of Aesthetic Response,* Baltimore and London: Johns Hopkins Univ. Press, 1978.

— *The Implied Reader,* Baltimore and London: Johns Hopkins Univ. Press, 1974.

JAEN, DIDIER T.: «La ambigüedad moral del *Lazarillo de Tormes*», *PMLA,* LXXXIII (1968), 130-134.

JAUSS, HANS ROBERT: «Literary History as a Challenge to Literary Theory», *New Literary History,* II, no. 1 (1970-1971), 7-31.

— «Levels of Identification of Hero and Audience», *New Literary History,* V (Winter 1974), 283-317.

JENNY, LAURENT: «La Stratégie de la Forme», *Poetique,* 27 (1976), 257-281.

JOHNSON, CARROLL B.: «El Buscón: D. Pablos, D. Diego, y D. Francisco», *Hispanófila,* 17 (1974), 1-26.

— *Inside Guzmán de Alfarache,* Berkeley, Los Angeles, and London: Univ. of California Press, 1978.

— «Mateo Alemán y sus fuentes literarias», *NRFH,* 28 (1979), 360-374.

KER, W. P.: *Epic and Romance,* 1980; rpt. New York: Dover Publications, 1957.

KERMODE, FRANK: *The Sense of an Ending,* New York: Oxford Univ. Press, 1966.

KERNAN, ALVIN B.: *The Plot of Satire,* New Haven and London: Yale Univ. Press, 1965.

KRISTEVA, JULIA: *Le Texte du Roman,* The Hague and Paris: Mouton, 1970.

— *Semiotikè: Recherches pour une sémanalyse,* Paris: Seuil, 1969.

KUENZLI, RUDOLF E.: «The Intersubjective Structure of the Reading Process: A Communication-Oriented Theory of Literature», *Diacritics* (June 1980), 47-74.

116

LACAN, JACQUES: *The Language of the Self*, trans. Anthony Wilden, 1956; rpt. New York: Dell, 1968.

LAING, R. D.: *The Divided Self*, 1959; rpt. Baltimore: Penguin Books, 1965.

LANGER, SUZANNE: *Feeling and Form*, New York: Scribner, 1953.

LAURENTI, JOSEPH L.: *Bibliografía de la literatura picaresca*, Metuchen, N. J.: Scarecrow Press, 1973.

— *Los Prólogos en las Novelas Picarescas*, Valencia: Artes Gráficas Soler, 1971.

La Vida de Lazarillo de Tormes, ed. Claudio Guillén, New York: Dell, 1966.

La Vida de Lazarillo de Tormes, ed. Alberto Blecua, Madrid: Clásicos Castalia, 1972.

LÁZARO CARRETER, FERNANDO: «Construcción y Sentido del *L. de T.*», *Ábaco*, 1 (1969), 45-134.

— «Glosas críticas a los *Pícaros en la literatura* de Alexander A. Parker», *HR*, 41 (1973), 469-497.

— *Lazarillo de Tormes en la picaresca*, Barcelona: Ariel, 1972.

— «Originalidad del Buscón», in *Estilo barroco y personalidad creadora*, Salamanca: Anaya, 1966.

LENTRICCHIA, FRANK: *After the New Criticism*, Chicago: Univ. of Chicago Press, 1980.

LIDA, RAIMUNDO: «Estilística. Un estudio sobre Quevedo», *Sur*, 4 (1931), 163-172.

— «Sobre el arte verbal del *Buscón*», *Philological Quarterly*, 51, No. 1 (1972), 255-269.

— «Pablos de Segovia y su agudeza», in *Homenaje a Casalduero*. Eds. Rizel Pincus Sigele and Gonzalo Sobejano, Madrid: Gredos, 1972.

LOMAX, DEREK W.: «On Re-Reading the *Lazarillo de Tormes*», in *Studia Iberica: Festschrift für Hans Flasche*. Eds. Carl-Hermann Körner and Klaus Ruhl, Bern, München: Francke, 1973.

MANCING, HOWARD: «The Deceptiveness of Lazarillo de Tormes», *PMLA*, 90 (May 1975), 426-432.

— «The Picaresque Novel: A Protean Form», *College Literature*, VI (1979-1980), 182-204.

MÁRQUEZ VILLANUEVA, FRANCISCO: «La actitud espiritual del *Lazarillo de Tormes*», in *Espiritualidad y literatura en el Siglo XVI*, Madrid: Alfaguara, 1968, 69-113.

MAY, T. E.: «Good and Evil in the *Buscón*: A Survey», *MLR*, 45 (1950), 319-335.

MCGRADY, DONALD: *Mateo Alemán*, New York: Twayne, 1968.

MOLHO, MAURICE: *Introducción al pensamiento picaresco*, trans. Gálvez-Cañero y Pidal, Salamanca: Anaya, 1972.

MONTE, ALBERTO DEL: *Itinerario de la novela picaresca española*, trans. E. Sordo, Barcelona: Lumen, 1971.

NORVAL, M. N.: «Original Sin and the 'Conversión' in *Guzmán de Alfarache*», *BHS*, 51 (1974), 346-364.

OLSEN, STEIN HAUGOM: *The Structure of Literary Understanding*, Cambridge, England: Cambridge Univ. Press, 1978.

ONG, WALTER J.: «The Writer's Audience is Always a Fiction», *PMLA*, 90 (1975), 9-21.

ORGEL, STEPHEN, and LYTLE, GUY, eds.: *Patronage in the Renaissance*, Princeton: Princeton Univ. Press, 1981.

PARKER, ALEXANDER: *Literature and the Delinquent*, Edinburgh: The University Press, 1967; translated as *Los Pícaros en la Literatura*, Madrid: Gredos, 1971.

PARR, JAMES: «La estructura satírica del Lazarillo», in *La Picaresca: Orígenes, Textos y Estructuras*, ed. Manuel Criado de Val, Madrid: Fundación Universitaria Española, 1979, 13-18.

PAULSON, RONALD: *The Fictions of Satire*, Baltimore: Johns Hopkins, Univ. Press, 1967.

117

PEALE, C. GEORGE: «*Guzmán de Alfarache* como discurso oral», *Journal of Hispanic Philology*, 4 (1979), 25-27.

PERRY, MARY ELIZABETH: *Crime and Society in Early Modern Seville*, Hanover, N. H. and London: Univ. Press of New England, 1980.

PORQUERAS MAYO, ALBERTO: *El prólogo como género literario. Su estilo en el Siglo de Oro español*, Madrid: C.S.I.C., 1957.

POULET, GEORGES: *The Interior Distance*, trans. Elliott Coleman, 1952; rpt. Ann Arbor: Univ. of Michigan Press, 1964.

PRINCE, GERALD: «Introduction to the Study of the Narratee», in *Reader Response Criticism*. Ed. Jane Tompkins, Baltimore and London: Johns Hopkins Univ. Press, 1980, 7-25.

QUEVEDO, FRANCISCO DE: *La Vida del Buscón llamado Pablos*, Introduction and Critical Edition of Fernando Lázaro Carreter, Salamanca: Consejo Superior de Investigaciones Científicas, 1965.

REED, WALTER L.: *An Exemplary History of the Novel: The Quixotic versus the Picaresque*, Chicago and London: Univ. of Chicago Press, 1981.

REY, ALFONSO: «La novela picaresca y el narrador fidedigno», *HR* (Winter 1979), 55-75.

RICO, FRANCISCO: *La novela picaresca y el punto de vista*, 1969; rpt. Barcelona: Editorial Seix Barral, 1976.

— *La Novela Picaresca Española*, Barcelona: Planeta, 1967.

RILEY, E. C.: *Cervantes' Theory of the Novel*, Oxford: Clarendon Press, 1962.

RIQUELME, JOHN PAUL: «The Ambivalence of Reading», *Diacritics* (June 1980), 75-86.

ROSA LIDA, MARÍA: «Función del cuento popular en *Lazarillo de Tormes*», *APICH* (1964), 349-359.

RUMEAU, A.: «Notes au Lazarillo», *BH*, LXVI (1964), 257-293.

SABAT DE RIVERS, GEORGINA: «La moral que Lázaro nos propone», *MLN*, 95 (1980), 233-251.

SAN MIGUEL, ANGEL: *Sentido y estructura del «Guzmán de Alfarache»*, Madrid: Gredos, 1971.

SARDUY, SEVERO: «El barroco y el neobarroco», in *América Latina en su Literatura*, ed. César Fernández Moreno, 3d. ed., 1972; rpt. México: Siglo Veintiuno, 1976.

SHLONSKY, TUVIA: «Literary Parody: Remarks on its Method and Function», *Proceedings of the AILC/ICLA*, IV, vol. 2, 797-801.

SERRANO PONCELA, SEGUNDO: «*El Buscón*, ¿parodia picaresca?», in *Del Romancero a Machado*, Caracas: Ediciones de la Biblioteca, Universidad Central de Venezuela, 1962.

SHIPLEY, GEORGE: «A Case of Functional Obscurity: the Master Tambourine-Painter of *Lazarillo*, Tratado VI», *MLN*, 97 (1982), 225-253.

— «Making the Case against Lázaro de Tormes», *PMLA*, 97 (March 1982), 179-194.

SICROFF, ALBERT A.: «Sobre el estilo de *Lazarillo de Tormes*», *NRFH*, 11 (1957), 157-170.

SIEBER, HARRY: «Apostrophes in the Buscón: An Approach to Quevedo's Narrative Technique», *MLN*, 83 (1968), 181-184.

— *Language and Society in «La Vida de Lazarillo de Tormes»*, Baltimore and London: Johns Hopkins Univ. Press, 1978.

— *The Picaresque*, London: Methuen, 1977.

SILVERMAN, JOSEPH H.: «Plinio, Pedro Mejía y Mateo Alemán: La enemistad entre las especies hecha símbolo visual», *Et Caetera*, 14 (1969), 23-31.

SMITH, BARBARA HERNSTEIN: *On the Margins of Discourse*, Chicago: Univ. of Chicago Press, 1978.

SOBEJANO, GONZALO, ed.: *Francisco de Quevedo. El Escritor y la Crítica*, Madrid: Taurus, 1978.

SOUBEROUX, JACQUES: «Pauvreté et Marginalité», *Imprévue* (1980-1981), 9-21.
SPITZER, LEO: *L'art de Quevedo dans le Buscón*, trans. M. and Mme. Dauer, Paris: Ediciones Hispano-americanas, 1972.
SULEIMAN, SUSAN R., and CROSSMAN, INGE, eds.: *The Reader in the Text. Essays on Audience and Interpretation*, Princeton: Princeton Univ. Press, 1980.
SYPHER, WYLIE: *Comedy*, Baltimore: Johns Hopkins Univ. Press, 1956.
TALÉNS, JENARO: *Novela picaresca y práctica de la transgresión*, Madrid: Ediciones Júcar, 1975.
TARR, F. COURTNEY: «Literary and Artistic Unity in the *Lazarillo de Tormes*», *PMLA*, XLII (1927), 404-421.
TODOROV, TZVETAN: *The Poetics of Prose*, trans. Richard Howard, Ithaca: Cornell University Press, 1971.
TOMPKINS, JANE P., ed.: *Reader-Response Criticism*, Baltimore and London: Johns Hopkins University Press, 1980.
TRUMAN, R. W.: «Lázaro de Tormes and the 'Homo Novus' Tradition», *MLR*, 64 (1969), 62-67.
UNAMUNO, MIGUEL DE: *Vida de Don Quijote y Sancho*, 6th ed., Buenos Aires and México: Espasa-Calpe Argentina, 1945.
VALBUENA PRATT, ANGEL: *La novela picaresca española*, Madrid: Aguilar, 1968.
VEGA, LOPE DE: *Arte nuevo de hacer comedias: La discreta enamorada*, 3d. ed., Madrid: Espasa-Calpe, 1948.
VERDAASDONK, H., and VAN REES, C. J.: «Reading a Text vs. Analyzing a Text», *Poetics*, 6, No. 1 (March 1977), 55-76.
VINAVER, EUGENE: *The Rise of Romance*, New York and London: Oxford Univ. Press, 1971.
VITZ, EVELYN BIRGE: «La Vie de Saint Alexis: Narrative Analysis and the Quest for the Sacred Subject», *PMLA*, 93 (May 1978), 396-498.
WARDROPPER, BRUCE: «El trastorno de la moral en *L. de T.*», *NRFH*, 15 (1961), 441-447.
WATT, IAN: *The Rise of the Novel*, Berkeley and Los Angeles: University of California Press, 1967.
WEBER, ALISON: «Cuatro clases de narrativa picaresca», in *La Picaresca: Orígenes, Textos y Estructuras*, ed. Manuel Criado de Val, Madrid: Fundación Universitaria Española, 1979, 13-18.
WEINBERG, BERNARD: *History of Literary Criticism in the Italian Renaissance*, Chicago: Univ. of Chicago Press, 1961.
WEINSTEIN, ARNOLD: *Fictions of the Self: 1550-1800*, Princeton: Princeton Univ. Press, 1981.
WEISSTEIN, ULRICH: *Comparative Literature and Literary Theory*, Bloomington and London: Indiana Univ. Press, 1973.
— «Parody, Travesty, and Burlesque: Imitations with a Vengeance», in *Actes du IV Congres de L'Association Internationale de Littérature Comparée*, The Hague and Paris: Mouton, 1966, 802-811.
WELLEK, RENÉ, and WARREN, AUSTIN: *Theory of Literature*, 3d ed., 1963; rpt. London: Penguin, 1976.
WHINNOM, KEITH: «The Problem of the 'Best-seller' in Spanish Golden-Age Literature», *BHS*, LVII (1980), 189-198.
WICKS, ULRICH: «Pícaro, Picaresque: The Picaresque in Literary Scholarship», *Genre*, 5 (1972), 153-192.
— «The Nature of Picaresque Narrative: A Modal Approach», *PMLA*, 89 (1974), 240-249.
— «The Romance of the Picaresque», *Genre*, XXI (1978), 29-44.

WILLIAMSON, EDWIN: «The Conflict between Author and Protagonist in Quevedo's *Buscón*», *Journal of Hispanic Philology*, 2 (1972), 45-60.

WOODS, M. J.: «Pitfalls for the Moralizer in *Lazarillo de Tormes*», *MLR*, LXXIV (1979), 580-598.

— «The Teasing Opening of *Guzmán de Alfarache*», *BHS*, LVII (1980), 213-218.

WOODWARD, L. J.: «Author-Reader Relationship in the *Lazarillo de Tormes*», *Forum for Modern Language Studies*, I (1965), 243-253.

ZUMTHOR, PAUL: «Le carrefour des Rhetoriquers», *Poétique*, 27 (1976), 320-336.